NIST Special Publication 800-40
Version 2.0

Creating a Patch and Vulnerability Management Program

Recommendations of the National Institute of Standards and Technology

Peter Mell
Tiffany Bergeron
David Henning

COMPUTER SECURITY

Computer Security Division
Information Technology Laboratory
National Institute of Standards and Technology
Gaithersburg, MD 20899-8930

November 2005

U.S. Department of Commerce

    Carlos M. Gutierrez, Secretary

Technology Administration

    Michelle O'Neill, Acting Under Secretary of Commerce for Technology

National Institute of Standards and Technology

    William A. Jeffrey, Director

Reports on Computer Systems Technology

The Information Technology Laboratory (ITL) at the National Institute of Standards and Technology (NIST) promotes the U.S. economy and public welfare by providing technical leadership for the nation's measurement and standards infrastructure. ITL develops tests, test methods, reference data, proof of concept implementations, and technical analysis to advance the development and productive use of information technology. ITL's responsibilities include the development of technical, physical, administrative, and management standards and guidelines for the cost-effective security and privacy of sensitive unclassified information in Federal computer systems. This Special Publication 800-series reports on ITL's research, guidance, and outreach efforts in computer security and its collaborative activities with industry, government, and academic organizations.

> Certain commercial entities, equipment, or materials may be identified in this document in order to describe an experimental procedure or concept adequately. Such identification is not intended to imply recommendation or endorsement by the National Institute of Standards and Technology, nor is it intended to imply that the entities, materials, or equipment are necessarily the best available for the purpose.

Acknowledgments

The authors, Peter Mell of NIST, Tiffany Bergeron of The MITRE Corporation, and David Henning of Hughes Network Systems, LLC, wish to express their thanks to Rob Pate of the United States Computer Emergency Readiness Team (US-CERT) for providing support for this publication. In addition, the authors would like to thank Miles Tracy of the U.S. Federal Reserve System, who co-authored the original version of the publication and provided significant input for this version, and Tanyette Miller of Booz Allen Hamilton, who put together the patching resources found in the appendices. The authors would also like to express their thanks to Timothy Grance of NIST, Manuel Costa and Todd Wittbold of The MITRE Corporation, Matthew Baum of the Corporation for National and Community Service, and Karen Kent of Booz Allen Hamilton for their insightful reviews, and to representatives from Department of Health and Human Services, Department of State, Environmental Protection Agency, Federal Reserve Board, and PatchAdvisor for their particularly valuable comments and suggestions.

Trademark Information

Microsoft and Windows are either registered trademarks or trademarks of Microsoft Corporation in the United States and other countries.

All other names are registered trademarks or trademarks of their respective companies.

Table of Contents

Executive Summary ES-1

1. **Introduction** 1-1
   1.1 Authority 1-1
   1.2 Purpose and Scope 1-1
   1.3 Audience 1-1
   1.4 Background Information 1-1
   1.5 Document Structure 1-3

2. **Patch and Vulnerability Management Process** 2-1
   2.1 Recommended Process 2-1
       2.1.1 The Patch and Vulnerability Group 2-1
       2.1.2 System Administrators 2-3
   2.2 Creating a System Inventory 2-3
       2.2.1 IT Inventory 2-3
       2.2.2 Grouping and Prioritizing Information Technology Resources 2-5
       2.2.3 Use of the IT Inventory and Scope of Related Duties 2-6
   2.3 Monitoring for Vulnerabilities, Remediations, and Threats 2-7
       2.3.1 Types of Security Concerns 2-7
       2.3.2 Monitoring Vulnerabilities, Remediations, and Threats 2-7
   2.4 Prioritizing Vulnerability Remediation 2-8
   2.5 Creating an Organization-Specific Remediation Database 2-9
   2.6 Testing Remediations 2-9
   2.7 Deploying Vulnerability Remediations 2-11
   2.8 Distributing Vulnerability and Remediation Information to Administrators 2-12
   2.9 Verifying Remediation 2-13
       2.9.1 Performing Vulnerability Scanning 2-13
       2.9.2 Reviewing Patch Logs 2-14
       2.9.3 Checking Patch Levels 2-15
   2.10 Vulnerability Remediation Training 2-15
   2.11 Recommendations 2-15

3. **Security Metrics for Patch and Vulnerability Management** 3-1
   3.1 Implementing Security Metrics with NIST SP 800-55 3-1
   3.2 Metrics Development 3-1
       3.2.1 Types of Patch and Vulnerability Metrics 3-1
       3.2.2 Targeting Metrics Towards Program Maturity 3-5
       3.2.3 Patch and Vulnerability Metrics Table 3-7
       3.2.4 Documenting and Standardizing Metrics 3-7
       3.2.5 Performance Targets and Cost Effectiveness 3-7
   3.3 Metrics Program Implementation 3-8
       3.3.1 Starting From Scratch 3-8
       3.3.2 False Positives and False Negatives 3-8
   3.4 Recommendations 3-8

4. **Patch and Vulnerability Management Issues** 4-1
   4.1 Enterprise Patching Solutions 4-1
       4.1.1 Types of Patching Solutions 4-1
       4.1.2 Security Risks 4-3

  4.1.3 Integrated Software Inventory Capabilities 4-4
  4.1.4 Integrated Vulnerability Scanning Capabilities 4-4
  4.1.5 Deployment Strategies 4-5
 4.2 Reducing the Need to Patch Through Smart Purchasing 4-5
 4.3 Using Standardized Configurations 4-6
 4.4 Patching After a Security Compromise 4-7
 4.5 Recommendations 4-7

5. United States Government Patching and Vulnerability Resources 5-1

 5.1 US-CERT National Cyber Alert System 5-1
 5.2 Common Vulnerabilities and Exposures Standard 5-1
 5.3 National Vulnerability Database 5-2
 5.4 US-CERT Vulnerability Notes Database 5-2
 5.5 Open Vulnerability Assessment Language 5-2
 5.6 Recommendations 5-2

6. Conclusion and Summary of Major Recommendations 6-1

List of Appendices

Appendix A— Acronyms A-1
Appendix B— Glossary B-1
Appendix C— Patch and Vulnerability Resource Types C-1

 C.1 Vendor Web Sites and Mailing Lists C-1
 C.2 Third-Party Web Sites C-2
 C.3 Third-Party Mailing Lists and Newsgroups C-2
 C.4 Vulnerability Scanners C-3
 C.5 Vulnerability Databases C-4
 C.6 Enterprise Patch Management Tools C-4
 C.7 Other Notification Tools C-5

Appendix D— Patch and Vulnerability Resources D-1
Appendix E— Index E-1

List of Figures

Figure 3-1. Maturity Levels for System Metrics 3-6

List of Tables

Table 3-1. Patch and Vulnerability Metrics 3-7

Executive Summary

Patch and vulnerability management is a security practice designed to proactively prevent the exploitation of IT vulnerabilities that exist within an organization. The expected result is to reduce the time and money spent dealing with vulnerabilities and exploitation of those vulnerabilities. Proactively managing vulnerabilities of systems will reduce or eliminate the potential for exploitation and involve considerably less time and effort than responding after an exploitation has occurred.

Patches are additional pieces of code developed to address problems (commonly called "bugs") in software. Patches enable additional functionality or address security flaws within a program. Vulnerabilities are flaws that can be exploited by a malicious entity to gain greater access or privileges than it is authorized to have on a computer system. Not all vulnerabilities have related patches; thus, system administrators must not only be aware of applicable vulnerabilities and available patches, but also other methods of remediation (e.g., device or network configuration changes, employee training) that limit the exposure of systems to vulnerabilities.

This document provides guidance on creating a security patch and vulnerability management program and testing the effectiveness of that program. The primary audience is security managers who are responsible for designing and implementing the program. However, this document also contains information useful to system administrators and operations personnel who are responsible for applying patches and deploying solutions (i.e., information related to testing patches and enterprise patching software).

Timely patching of security issues is generally recognized as critical to maintaining the operational availability, confidentiality, and integrity of information technology (IT) systems. However, failure to keep operating system and application software patched is one of the most common issues identified by security and IT professionals. New patches are released daily, and it is often difficult for even experienced system administrators to keep abreast of all the new patches and ensure proper deployment in a timely manner. Most major attacks in the past few years have targeted known vulnerabilities for which patches existed before the outbreaks. Indeed, the moment a patch is released, attackers make a concerted effort to reverse engineer the patch swiftly (measured in days or even hours), identify the vulnerability, and develop and release exploit code. Thus, the time immediately after the release of a patch is ironically a particularly vulnerable moment for most organizations due to the time lag in obtaining, testing, and deploying a patch.

To help address this growing problem, it is recommended that all organizations have a systematic, accountable, and documented process for managing exposure to vulnerabilities through the timely deployment of patches. This document describes the principles and methodologies organizations can use to accomplish this. Organizations should be aware that applying patches and mitigating vulnerabilities is not a straightforward process, even in organizations that utilize a formal patch and vulnerability management process. To help with the operational issues related to patch application, this document covers areas such as prioritizing, obtaining, testing, and applying patches. It also discusses testing the effectiveness of the patching program and suggests a variety of metrics for that purpose.

NIST recommends that Federal agencies implement the following recommendations to assist in patch and vulnerability management. Personnel responsible for these duties should read the corresponding sections of the document to ensure they have an adequate understanding of important related issues.

Organizations should create a patch and vulnerability group (PVG) to facilitate the identification and distribution of patches within the organization.

The PVG should be specially tasked to implement the patch and vulnerability management program throughout the organization. The PVG is the central point for vulnerability remediation efforts, such as OS and application patching and configuration changes. Since the PVG needs to work actively with local administrators, large organizations may need to have several PVGs; they could work together or be structured hierarchically with an authoritative top-level PVG. The duties of a PVG should include the following:

1. Inventory the organization's IT resources to determine which hardware equipment, operating systems, and software applications are used within the organization.

2. Monitor security sources for vulnerability announcements, patch and non-patch remediations, and emerging threats that correspond to the software within the PVG's system inventory.

3. Prioritize the order in which the organization addresses remediating vulnerabilities.

4. Create a database of remediations that need to be applied to the organization.

5. Conduct testing of patches and non-patch remediations on IT devices that use standardized configurations.

6. Oversee vulnerability remediation.

7. Distribute vulnerability and remediation information to local administrators.

8. Perform automated deployment of patches to IT devices using enterprise patch management tools.

9. Configure automatic update of applications whenever possible and appropriate.

10. Verify vulnerability remediation through network and host vulnerability scanning.

11. Train administrators on how to apply vulnerability remediations.

Organizations should use automated patch management tools to expedite the distribution of patches to systems.

Widespread manual patching of computers is becoming ineffective as the number of patches that need to be installed grows and as attackers continue to develop exploit code more rapidly. While patching and vulnerability monitoring can often appear an overwhelming task, consistent mitigation of organizational vulnerabilities can be achieved through a tested and integrated patching process that makes efficient use of automated patching technology. Enterprise patch management tools allow the PVG, or a group they work closely with, to automatically push patches out to many computers quickly. All moderate to large organizations should be using enterprise patch management tools for the majority of their computers. Even small organizations should be migrating to some form of automated patching tool.

Organizations should deploy enterprise patch management tools using a phased approach.

Implementing patch management tools in phases allows process and user communication issues to be addressed with a small group before deploying the patch application universally. Most organizations deploy patch management tools first to standardized desktop systems and single-platform server farms of similarly configured servers. Once this has been accomplished, organizations should address the more difficult issue of integrating multiplatform environments, nonstandard desktop systems, legacy computers, and computers with unusual configurations. Manual methods may need to be used for operating systems and applications not supported by automated patching tools, as well as some computers with unusual configurations; examples include embedded systems, industrial control systems, medical devices, and experimental systems. For such computers, there should be a written and implemented procedure for the manual patching process, and the PVG should coordinate local administrator efforts.

Organizations should assess and mitigate the risks associated with deploying enterprise patch management tools.

Although enterprise patch management tools can be very effective at reducing risk, they can also create additional security risks for an organization. For example, an attacker could break into the central patch management computer and use the enterprise patch management tool as a way to distribute malicious code efficiently. Organizations should partially mitigate these risks through the application of standard security techniques that should be used when deploying any enterprise-wide application.

Organizations should consider using standardized configurations for IT resources.

Having standardized configurations within the IT enterprise will reduce the labor related to patch and vulnerability management. Organizations with standardized configurations will find it much easier and less costly to implement a patch and vulnerability management program. Also, the PVG may not be able to test patches adequately if IT devices use nonstandard configurations. Enterprise patch management tools may be ineffective if deployed within an environment where every IT device is configured uniquely, because the side effects of the various patches on the different configurations will be unknown. Comprehensive patch and vulnerability management is almost impossible within large organizations that do not deploy standard configurations. Organizations should focus standardization efforts on the types of IT resources that make up a significant portion of their IT resources. NIST Special Publication 800-70, *Security Configuration Checklists Program for IT Products—Guidance for Checklists Users and Developers*, provides guidance on creating and using security configuration checklists, which are helpful tools for standardization.

Organizations should consistently measure the effectiveness of their patch and vulnerability management program and apply corrective actions as necessary.

Patch and vulnerability metrics fall into three categories: susceptibility to attack, mitigation response time, and cost, which includes a metric for the business impact of program failures. The emphasis on patch and vulnerability metrics being taken for a system or IT security program should reflect the patch and vulnerability management maturity level. For example, attack susceptibility metrics such as the number of patches, vulnerabilities, and network services per system are generally more useful for a program with a low maturity level than a high maturity level. Organizations should document what metrics will be taken for each system and the details of each of those metrics. Realistic performance targets for each metric should be communicated to system owners and system security officers. Once these targets have been achieved, more ambitious targets can be set. It is important to carefully raise the bar on patch and vulnerability security to avoid overwhelming system security officers and system administrators.

1. Introduction

1.1 Authority

The National Institute of Standards and Technology (NIST) developed this document in furtherance of its statutory responsibilities under the Federal Information Security Management Act (FISMA) of 2002, Public Law 107-347.

NIST is responsible for developing standards and guidelines, including minimum requirements, for providing adequate information security for all agency systems;[1] but such standards and guidelines shall not apply to national security systems. This guideline is consistent with the requirements of the Office of Management and Budget (OMB) Circular A-130, Section 8b(3), "Securing Agency Information Systems," as analyzed in A-130, Appendix IV: Analysis of Key Sections. Supplemental information is provided in A-130, Appendix III.

This guideline has been prepared for use by Federal agencies. It may be used by nongovernmental organizations on a voluntary basis and is not subject to copyright, though attribution is desired.

Nothing in this document should be taken to contradict standards and guidelines made mandatory and binding on Federal agencies by the Secretary of Commerce under statutory authority, nor should these guidelines be interpreted as altering or superseding the existing authorities of the Secretary of Commerce, Director of the OMB, or any other Federal official.

1.2 Purpose and Scope

This publication is designed to assist organizations in implementing security patch and vulnerability remediation programs. It focuses on how to create an organizational process and test the effectiveness of the process. It also seeks to inform the reader about the technical solutions that are available for vulnerability remediation.

1.3 Audience

This document is intended to be used primarily by security managers responsible for designing and implementing security patch and vulnerability remediation programs. However, it also contains information of use to system administrators and security operations personnel who are responsible for applying patches and deploying solutions (e.g., information on testing patches and enterprise patching software).

1.4 Background Information

From July 2003 through June 2005, the average number of published computer vulnerabilities was 2513 per year, or nearly seven each day.[2] Even a small organization with a single server can expect to spend time reviewing a handful of critical patches per month. This stream of vulnerabilities has resulted in systems constantly being threatened by new attacks.

---

[1] The word "systems" refers to a set of information technology (IT) assets, processes, applications, and related IT resources that are under the same direct management and budgetary control; have the same function or mission objective; have essentially the same security needs; and reside in the same general operating environment. All IT systems are either of the type "General Support" or "Major Application" as specified by NIST Special Publication 800-18.

[2] The source for this information is the National Vulnerability Database, which is available at http://nvd.nist.gov/.

The level of damage caused by an attack can be quite severe. A number of Internet worms (self-propagating code that exploits vulnerabilities over the Internet) such as Code Red, Nimda, Blaster, and MyDoom have been released in recent years. There are some common data points for these worm outbreaks. First, as the authors of worm code have gotten more sophisticated, the worms have been able to spread faster than their predecessors. Second, they each hit hundreds of thousands of computers worldwide. Most importantly, each one of them attacked a known vulnerability for which a patch or other mitigation steps had already been released.[3] Each major outbreak was preventable.

Benjamin Franklin once said that "an ounce of prevention equals a pound of cure." Patch and vulnerability management is the "ounce of prevention" compared to the "pound of cure" that is incident response. The decision on how and when to mitigate via patching or other remediation methods should come from a comparison of time, resources, and money to be spent. For example, assume that a new computer worm is released that can spread rapidly and damage any workstation in the organization unless it is stopped. The potential cost to not mitigate is described by the following equation:

Cost not to mitigate = W * T * R, where (W) is the number of workstations, (T) is the time spent fixing systems or lost in productivity, and (R) is the hourly rate of the time spent.[4]

For an organization where there are 1000 computers to be fixed, each taking an average of 8 hours of downtime (4 hours for one worker to rebuild a system, plus 4 hours the computer owner is without a computer to do work) at a rate of $70/hour for wages and benefits:

1000 computers * 8 hours * $70/hour = $560,000 to respond after an attack.

Compare this to the cost of manual monitoring and prevention. Assume the vulnerability exploited by the worm and the corresponding patch are announced in advance of the worm being created. This has been accurate for exploits historically, as true zero day attacks are not frequent. Manually monitoring for new patches for a single workstation type takes as little as 10 minutes each day, or 60.8 hours/year. Applying a workstation patch generally takes no more than 10 minutes. This makes the cost equation:

60.8 hours monitoring * $70/hour = $4,256 monitoring cost per year

0.16 hours patching * 1,000 computers @ $70/hour = $11,200 to manually apply each patch

Total cost to maintain the systems = $4,256 + $11,200/patch.

For any single vulnerability for which a widespread worm will be created, manual monitoring and patching is much more cost-effective than responding to a worm infection. However, given that patches are constantly released, manual patching becomes prohibitively expensive unless the operating environment consists of only a few software packages (thus decreasing the total number of patches needed) or the organization relies on end users to patch their systems (thus distributing the patching workload, but also introducing a need for patch installation oversight). Since few organizations use a small number of software packages or can rely on end users to effectively patch systems, widespread manual patching is not a cost-effective organizational approach.[5]

---

[3] Since the late 1990's, the length of time between the announcement of a new major vulnerability and the release of a new exploit has dropped from months to weeks or days.
[4] In addition to the costs identified through this formula, a security incident could also cause damage to an organization's reputation. This is most significant for organizations that are entrusted with sensitive information or operations. When determining the potential cost to not mitigate, an organization should consider the possible mpact to its reputation.
[5] Manual patching is still useful and necessary for many legacy and specialized systems.

A third option is to invest in an automated patching solution. These solutions automatically check for required patches and deploy them. Both free and commercial solutions are available. Assume that a commercial solution costs $15,000 and charges $20 per computer for annual maintenance. This approach will be much cheaper than the manual solution, even though it will be necessary to dedicate possibly an entire person to maintaining, updating, and patching using the automated solution.

> 40 hours/week * 52 weeks/year * $70/hour = $145,600/year for the administrator to run the patching solution

> $145,600 + 1,000 computers * $20/computer = $165,600 annual patching cost for the automated solution

It is not possible to save money by neglecting patch installation. It is extremely expensive to employ manual patching efforts and it is difficult to do it effectively. Therefore, NIST strongly recommends that all organizations make effective use of automated patching solutions.

1.5 Document Structure

The remainder of this document is organized into the following sections:

+ Section 2 explains a recommended management process for implementing a security patch and vulnerability remediation program.

+ Section 3 discusses security metrics to be used for measuring the success of a security patch and vulnerability remediation program.

+ Section 4 highlights various issues in managing a patch and vulnerability remediation program. In particular, this section focuses on enterprise patching solutions.

+ Section 5 provides a short discussion of United States government vulnerability and patching resources.

+ Section 6 summarizes the major conclusions of this publication.

The document also contains appendices with supporting material, as follows:

+ Appendix A presents common acronyms used throughout the document.

+ Appendix B provides a glossary of terminology used throughout the document.

+ Appendix C discusses common types of popular patching resources.

+ Appendix D lists popular patching resources.

+ Appendix E contains an index for the document.

2. Patch and Vulnerability Management Process

This section discusses a systematic approach to patch and vulnerability management. The approach is provided as a model that an organization should adapt to its environment as appropriate. Implementing such an approach is necessary to cost-effectively respond to the ever-growing number of vulnerabilities in IT systems.

2.1 Recommended Process

NIST recommends that organizations create a group of individuals, called the patch and vulnerability group (PVG), who are specially tasked to implement the patch and vulnerability management program. The PVG is the central point for vulnerability remediation efforts (e.g., patching and configuration changes). Since the PVG must actively work with local administrators, large organizations may need to have several PVGs. These PVGs could work together in a confederation or could be structured hierarchically with an authoritative top-level PVG. The remainder of this document is based on the assumption that there is only one PVG per organization.

As much as possible, the burden of implementing and testing remediations should be shifted from local administrators to the PVG. This should save money by eliminating duplication of effort (e.g., multiple system administrators testing the same patch on similar computers) and by enabling automated solutions, thereby avoiding costly manual installations. The easiest way to accomplish this is by implementing enterprise patching solutions that allow the PVG, or a group they work closely with, to automatically push patches out to many computers quickly. If automated patch management tools are not available, the PVG should coordinate local administrator efforts.

For the PVG to be able to adequately test automatically deployed patches, organizations should use standardized configurations for IT devices (e.g., desktop computers, routers, firewalls, servers) as much as possible. Enterprise patch management tools will be ineffective if deployed in an environment where every IT device is configured uniquely, because the side effects of the various patches will be unknown.

To implement a cost-effective PVG, the scope of the PVG must be well-defined. The PVG will monitor for and address only vulnerabilities and remediations applicable to IT technologies that are widely used within the organization.[6] This list of IT technologies will be carefully formulated and made available to all local administrators. The local administrators will be responsible for securing IT technologies that are not within the PVG scope. The PVG will provide assistance and training to local administrators in how to perform this function. The remainder of this section provides details on the roles and responsibilities of the PVG and system administrators.

2.1.1 The Patch and Vulnerability Group

The PVG should be a formal group that incorporates representatives from information security and operations. These representatives should include individuals with knowledge of vulnerability and patch management, as well as system administration, intrusion detection, and firewall management. In addition, it is helpful to have specialists in the operating systems and applications most used within the organization. Personnel who already provide system or network administration functions, perform vulnerability scanning, or operate intrusion detection systems are also likely candidates for the PVG.

---

[6] Some organizations might choose to have their PVG monitor for vulnerabilities and remediations for all IT technologies used within the organization. This is most feasible when the organization has a relatively small variety of IT technologies in use, or when the PVG uses an external vulnerability monitoring service (as described in Appendix C) that can monitor for all the necessary IT technologies on behalf of the PVG.

The size of the group and the amount of time devoted to PVG duties will vary broadly across various organizations. Much depends on the size and complexity of the organization, the size and complexity of its network, and its budget. The PVG of smaller organizations may be comprised of only one or two members, with a focus on critical vulnerabilities and systems. Regardless of the organization's size or resources, patch and vulnerability management can be accomplished with proper planning and process.

The duties of the PVG are outlined below. Subsequent sections discuss certain duties in more detail.

1. **Create a System Inventory.** The PVG should use existing inventories of the organization's IT resources to determine which hardware equipment, operating systems, and software applications are used within the organization. The PVG should also maintain a manual inventory of IT resources not captured in the existing inventories. Section 2.2 contains detailed guidance on creating an inventory.

2. **Monitor for Vulnerabilities, Remediations, and Threats.** The PVG is responsible for monitoring security sources for vulnerability announcements, patch and non-patch remediations, and emerging threats that correspond to the software within the PVG's system inventory. Section 2.3 discusses where and how to monitor for vulnerabilities, remediations, and threats.

3. **Prioritize Vulnerability Remediation.** The PVG should prioritize the order in which the organization addresses vulnerability remediation. Detailed information is contained in Section 2.4.

4. **Create an Organization-Specific Remediation Database.** The PVG should create a database of remediations that need to be applied to the organization. Section 2.5 contains additional information.

5. **Conduct Generic Testing of Remediations.** The PVG should be able to test patches and non-patch remediations on IT devices that use standardized configurations. This will avoid the need for local administrators to perform redundant testing. The PVG should also work closely with local administrators to test patches and configuration changes on important systems. Information on testing remediations is contained in Section 2.6.

6. **Deploy Vulnerability Remediations.** The PVG should oversee vulnerability remediation. Section 2.7 contains information on this process.

7. **Distribute Vulnerability and Remediation Information to Local Administrators.** The PVG is responsible for informing local administrators about vulnerabilities and remediations that correspond to software packages included within the PVG scope and that are in the organizational software inventory. More information is available in Section 2.8.

8. **Perform Automated Deployment of Patches.** The PVG should deploy patches automatically to IT devices using enterprise patch management tools. Alternately, the PVG could work closely with the group actually running the patch management tools. Automated patching tools allow an administrator to update hundreds or even thousands of systems from a single console. Deployment is fairly simple when there are homogeneous computing platforms, with standardized desktop systems and similarly configured servers. Multiplatform environments, nonstandard desktop systems, legacy computers, and computers with unusual configurations may also be integrated. Section 4.1 provides information about enterprise patching tools.

9. **Configure Automatic Update of Applications Whenever Possible and Appropriate.** Many newer applications provide a feature that checks the vendor's Web site for updates. This feature can be very useful in minimizing the level of effort required to identify, distribute, and install patches. However, some organizations may not wish to implement this feature because it might interfere with their configuration management process. A recommended option would be a locally distributed automated update process, where the patches are made available from the organization's network. Applications can then be updated from the local network instead of from the Internet. Section 4.1 discusses such tools in the context of enterprise patching tools in general.

10. **Verify Vulnerability Remediation Through Network and Host Vulnerability Scanning.** The PVG should verify that vulnerabilities have been successfully remediated. Section 2.9 provides information regarding remediation verification.

11. **Vulnerability Remediation Training.** The PVG should train administrators on how to apply vulnerability remediations. In organizations that rely on end users to patch computers, the PVG must also train users on this function. Section 0 provides further guidance.

2.1.2 System Administrators

System administrators are responsible for making sure that applicable IT resources follow the organization's standard configuration and that those resources are participating in the organization's automated patching system. If the organization is not using an automated patching system, system administrators must use the PVG as a primary resource for vulnerability remediation and work with the PVG on timeframes for remediation application. For IT resources that are outside of the PVG scope, system administrators are responsible for monitoring for vulnerabilities and remediations, testing those remediations, and applying remediations.

2.2 Creating a System Inventory

NIST recommends that the PVG use existing inventories of the organization's IT resources to determine which hardware equipment, operating systems, and software applications are used within the organization, and then group and prioritize those resources. The PVG should also maintain a manual inventory of IT resources not captured in the existing inventories. Having a system inventory and priority listing will enable the PVG to determine which hardware and software applications they will support by monitoring for vulnerabilities, patches, and threats, and will enable them to respond quickly and effectively.

2.2.1 IT Inventory

Before a system is accredited,[7] an inventory of all IT resources contained within the system should be created. This inventory should be updated regularly as part of the system's configuration management process. All IT resources within an organization must be assigned to a particular system such that the set of all systems covers all IT resources.

Creating and maintaining a separate inventory for each system may not be cost-effective. Therefore, organizations may prefer to maintain an organization-wide inventory containing all IT resources. This is perfectly acceptable (and in many cases recommended) as long as each IT resource is labeled such that it

---

[7] NIST Special Publication (SP) 800-37 contains detailed information on system accreditation. It is available at http://csrc.nist.gov/publications/nistpubs/800-37/SP800-37-final.pdf.

is associated with one and only one system. The capability to output the list of IT resources associated with each system must exist.[8]

Each organization must determine the proper level of abstraction for their inventory. For example, one organization may track what software is installed on each computer, while another organization may also track software version numbers. Organizations should carefully and deliberately choose their level of abstraction because sometimes collecting too much information is just as bad (or worse) than collecting too little. Organizations should determine what uses they will make of their inventory (in addition to patch management) and collect only the information needed for those uses.

The following is a sample list of items that an organization could include within their inventory (not all items will apply to all IT resources):

1. Associated system name
2. Property number
3. Owner of the IT resource (i.e., main user)
4. System administrator
5. Physical location
6. Connected network port
7. Software configuration
    a. Operating system and version number
    b. Software packages and version numbers
    c. Network services
    d. Internet Protocol (IP) address (if it is static)
8. Hardware configuration
    a. Central processing unit
    b. Memory
    c. Disk space
    d. Ethernet addresses (i.e., network cards)
    e. Wireless capability
    f. Input/output capability (e.g., Universal Serial Bus, Firewire)

---

[8] Organizations often have multiple inventories of IT resources. For example, some organizations use automated asset management software that inventories devices and the software each device runs. Organizations might also have inventories performed as part of business continuity planning and other efforts.

g. Firmware versions.

It is usually impractical to require people to enter this information manually for each IT resource. Organizations that try this approach may end up with inventories that contain large sets of IT resources that are inaccurate and updated infrequently. A more effective approach is to use commercially available automated inventory management tools whenever possible. These tools typically require organizations to install an agent on each computer. The agent then actively monitors changes in the computer's configuration and reports to a central database, thereby providing the PVG and management an accurate picture of a system's IT resources. Unfortunately, as good as the automated tools are, some information will always need to be manually keyed (e.g., physical location). An automated tool should provide the option to gather this information periodically by presenting users with forms to fill out.

2.2.2 Grouping and Prioritizing Information Technology Resources

The resources within the inventory should be grouped and assigned priority levels to facilitate remediation efforts. Resource grouping and prioritization is helpful in assessing risk to systems, and should be used to help identify which systems may require the special attention of the patch and vulnerability management program. The primary grouping should be by system name and the system's Federal Information Processing Standard (FIPS) 199 impact designation.[9] It may also be useful to group resources by network location. This is particularly important for those resources that are directly exposed to the Internet and those that reside behind internal high-security areas.

If this grouping and prioritization is not performed, organizations may embark upon unnecessarily costly remediation strategies. For example, when a new vulnerability is discovered within an organization that does not do remediation prioritization, system administrators might be instructed to patch all vulnerable computers immediately. This could result in a major disruption as system administrators stop all other work so they can patch computers. Even worse, the patch may be applied quickly without thorough testing, resulting in actual damage to the organization's systems. With prioritization, the organization may realize that a majority of the vulnerable computers could be patched over a period of time using the organization's standard configuration management process and patch testing procedures. The organization could then focus its immediate patching efforts on the vulnerable computers that are most at risk (e.g., possibly those directly exposed to the Internet).

2.2.2.1 NIST Special Publication 800-18

Guidance on grouping IT resources into officially designated and accredited systems is provided within NIST Special Publication (SP) 800-18.[10] It says that IT resources that are grouped within the same system should have the following characteristics:

+ The elements are under the same direct management control

+ The elements have the same function or mission objective

+ The elements have similar security operating characteristics and security needs

+ The elements exist in the same general operating environment.

---

[9] FIPS 199 is available for download at http://csrc.nist.gov/publications/fips/fips199/FIPS-PUB-199-final.pdf.
[10] NIST SP 800-18 is available at http://csrc.nist.gov/publications/nistpubs/800-18/Planguide.PDF.

2.2.2.2 Federal Information Processing Standard 199

FIPS 199 establishes security categories for Federal information and information systems. Other organizations may also apply these standards on an ad hoc basis or adopt a more formal approach. The categories are determined based on the potential impact of a loss of confidentiality, integrity, or availability of information or an information system. The security categories should be used to prioritize multi-system vulnerability remediation efforts.

2.2.2.3 Intersystem Prioritization

Use of FIPS 199 will provide helpful information for prioritizing remediation efforts between systems, but it is often also necessary to prioritize within a system boundary. The PVG and system personnel should document which IT resources are of higher priority within a given system. Common higher-priority resources often fall into one or more of the following categories:

+ Resources essential for system operation (e.g., servers)
+ Resources used for security management
+ Resources residing on the organization's network boundary
+ Resources that contain information of higher importance
+ Resources that are accessible to external users.

The inventory information can be used to help the PVG with this prioritization, and these prioritizations can then be stored in the inventory itself.

2.2.3 Use of the IT Inventory and Scope of Related Duties

The inventory is the foundation on which the PVG will conduct its operations, since it is the PVG's window into understanding the organization's IT configuration. The inventory will be used primarily to create a list of PVG-supported hardware equipment, operating systems, and software applications. It will also help the PVG and administrators to quickly respond to threats, and provide system personnel information to help them secure their systems.

2.2.3.1 List of Supported Resources

The PVG should define a set of hardware equipment, operating systems, and software applications that they will support. The PVG will then be responsible for monitoring information regarding vulnerabilities, patches, and threats corresponding to the supported hardware, operating systems, and applications. The PVG should clearly communicate the supported resources to system administrators so that the administrators know which hardware, operating systems, and applications the PVG will be checking for new patches, vulnerabilities, and threats. The list of supported resources should be created by analyzing the inventory and identifying those resources that are used within the organization. Hardware equipment, operating systems, and software applications used on high priority or sensitive systems or on a large number of systems should be included in the list. By publishing this list, the PVG will enable system administrators to know when or if they have an unsupported resource. System administrators should be taught how to independently monitor and remediate unsupported hardware equipment, operating systems, and software applications.

2.2.3.2 Providing System Personnel Inventory Information

The PVG should also give system owners, system security officers, and system administrators access to the inventory information.[11] This will help them better secure the organization's systems. However, system personnel should only have access to their own system inventory, since system inventory information is sensitive in nature. Giving system personnel access to the inventory is also important because maintaining the inventory will require the PVG to work closely with system personnel.

2.3 Monitoring for Vulnerabilities, Remediations, and Threats

The PVG is responsible for monitoring security sources for vulnerability announcements, patch and non-patch remediations, and threats that correspond to the software within the organizational software inventory. A variety of sources should be monitored to ensure that the PVG is aware of all newly discovered vulnerabilities.

2.3.1 Types of Security Concerns

The PVG is responsible for monitoring for vulnerabilities, remediations, and threats:

+ **Vulnerabilities.** Vulnerabilities are software flaws or misconfigurations that cause a weakness in the security of a system. Vulnerabilities can be exploited by a malicious entity to violate policies—for example, to gain greater access or permission than is authorized on a computer.

+ **Remediations.** There are three primary methods of remediation: installation of a software patch, adjustment of a configuration setting, and removal of affected software. Refer to Section 2.7 for further details regarding methods of remediation.

+ **Threats.** Threats are capabilities or methods of attack developed by malicious entities to exploit vulnerabilities and potentially cause harm to a computer system or network. Threats usually take the form of exploit scripts, worms, viruses, rootkits, and Trojan horses.

System administrators should monitor for vulnerabilities, remediations, and threats for systems under their control running software not contained in the organizational inventory.

2.3.2 Monitoring Vulnerabilities, Remediations, and Threats

There are several types of resources available for monitoring the status of vulnerabilities, remediations, and threats. Appendix D contains a partial listing of popular resources. Each type of resource has its own strengths and weaknesses. NIST recommends using more than one type of resource to ensure accurate and timely knowledge. The most common types of resources are as follows:

+ Vendor Web sites and mailing lists

+ Third-party Web sites

+ Third-party mailing lists and newsgroups

+ Vulnerability scanners

+ Vulnerability databases

---

[11] Typically, these parties already have access to existing inventories, but the PVG inventory might contain additional inventory information that is otherwise unavailable to the parties.

+ Enterprise patch management tools

+ Other notification tools.

Appendix C discusses in detail the advantages and disadvantages of the various types of resources for obtaining vulnerability, patch, and threat information.

Vendors are the authoritative source of information for patches related to their products. However, many vendors will not announce vulnerabilities in their products until patches are available; accordingly, monitoring third-party vulnerability resources as well is recommended. Enterprise patching tools usually provide lists of all patches available from supported vendors, which alleviate the PVG from constantly having to monitor a large number of vendor security Web sites and mailing lists.

NIST recommends that organizations monitor for vulnerabilities, remediation, and threats using the following resource types at a minimum:

+ Enterprise patch management tool, to obtain all available patches from supported vendors

+ Vendor security mailing lists and Web sites, to obtain all available patches from vendors not supported by the enterprise patch management tool

+ Vulnerability database or mailing list to obtain immediate information on all known vulnerabilities and suggested remediations (e.g., the National Vulnerability Database)

+ Third-party vulnerability mailing lists that highlight the most critical vulnerabilities (e.g., the US-CERT Cyber Security Alerts). Such lists will help organizations focus on the most important vulnerabilities that may get overlooked among the myriad of vulnerabilities published by more general vulnerability resources.

After initial assessment of a new vulnerability, remediation, or threat, the PVG should continue to monitor it for updates and new information. For example, a software vendor might release a new patch in place of a software reconfiguration it originally recommended as a temporary remediation measure. By performing ongoing monitoring for new information, the PVG would be aware of the new patch and could determine if it would provide a better solution than the software reconfiguration. Ongoing monitoring is also important because additional analysis of vulnerabilities might determine that they are more or less severe than previously thought.

2.4 Prioritizing Vulnerability Remediation

The PVG should consider each threat and its potential impact on the organization when setting priorities for vulnerability remediation. This evaluation would include the following:[12]

+ Determine the significance of the threat or vulnerability. Establish which systems are vulnerable or exposed, with a focus on those systems that are essential for operation, as well as other high-priority systems. Evaluate the impact on the systems, the organization, and network if the vulnerability is not removed and is exploited. Remember that the organization's security architecture may automatically mitigate certain threats, thus reducing the urgency to apply certain patches. For example, if the organization disables certain functionality within their browsers (e.g.

---

[12] The PVG is not expected to perform this evaluation on its own. System and network security officers and administrators might assist the PVG by assessing the impact of threats to individual systems, based on vulnerability, remediation, and threat information provided by the PVG.

scripting languages), then applying patches that fix vulnerabilities within those scripting languages is not a priority.

+ Determine the existence, extent, and spread of related worms, viruses, or exploits. Ascertain whether malicious code has been published and the level of distribution. Determine the damage caused, such as system access, information disclosure, arbitrary code execution, or denial of service. Organizations should assume that malicious individuals are in possession of exploit code for any vulnerability for which there is a patch, since patches are often reverse engineered quickly.

+ Determine the risks involved with applying the patch or non-patch remediation. Identify whether the fix will affect the functionality of other software applications or services through research and testing. Establish what degree of risk is acceptable.

The PVG should be aware of the resource constraints of local administrators and should attempt to avoid overwhelming them with a large number of patches or other remediations for identified vulnerabilities. With the exception of small IT deployments, it is a complex and difficult endeavor for local administrators to perform all remediations in a timely manner. This is attributed not only to time and resource constraints but also to the greater complexity and heterogeneity of systems in larger environments. Thus, setting priorities for which systems to patch in what order is essential for an effective patch process.

2.5 Creating an Organization-Specific Remediation Database

The PVG should create a database of remediations that need to be applied within the organization. Enterprise patch management tools usually supply such a database, but the PVG may need to manually maintain a separate one for IT technologies not supported by the patch management tool. Manually maintained databases should contain instructions on removing vulnerabilities by installing patches or performing workarounds, as well as the actual patches when applicable.[13] Whether automated or manual, databases should contain a copy of each patch for situations when the Internet may not be accessible or when the vendor's Web site may have been compromised. In addition, it is likely easier for local administrators to apply a patch using the PVG database as opposed to a vendor site that might overwhelm administrators with a large array of available patches. While the creation of a database is recommended, resource constraints may limit an organization to listing only Web sites or specific Uniform Resource Locators (URL) for each patch. Such a solution should be feasible when each hyperlink to a patch is associated with documented advice and timeframes from the PVG. While manually maintained databases may be possible, NIST strongly recommends purchasing automated patching products that inherently contain such databases.

2.6 Testing Remediations

If an organization uses standardized host configurations, the PVG will be able to test patches and non-patch remediations on those configurations. This will avoid the need for redundant testing by each local system administrator. System administrators are responsible for testing patches and non-patch remediations to mitigate vulnerabilities and threats identified for software not monitored by the PVG.

---

[13] Organizations might also find it helpful to have the PVG write a threat assessment summary for the most significant vulnerabilities and patches, then distribute the summary to local administrators and management or make it available through the remediation database. The summary should be helpful in ensuring that people understand the importance of performing the remediation and the possible consequences of not doing so.

Precautions should be taken before applying the identified patch or non-patch remediation. Remediation testing guidelines may include the following:

+ Most vendors provide some type of authentication mechanism. The downloaded patch should be checked against any of the authenticity methods the vendor provides, including cryptographic checksums, Pretty Good Privacy (PGP) signatures, and digital certificates. Some of these methods, such as verifying digital signatures, are highly automated, requiring little user interaction. Others, such as SHA-1 or MD5 checksums, require the user to visit the vendor's Web site to compare the checksum listed there against the checksum for the downloaded patch.[14] Although these methods add another level of authentication, they are not foolproof.

+ A virus scan should also be run on all patches before installation. Before running the scan, the PVG or system administrator should ensure that the virus signature database in the antivirus program is up to date. Again, this system is not foolproof. For example, if an attacker has created an entirely new Trojan horse and included it with the patch, it might not be detected by the virus scan.

+ Patches and configuration modifications should be tested on non-production systems since remediation can easily produce unintended consequences.[15] Many patches are extremely complicated and can affect many portions of a system, since they often replace system files and alter security settings.[16] Patches may also include fixes for multiple vulnerabilities or contain non-security changes, such as new functionality. In addition, patches and configuration changes are often released in haste to repair a vulnerability quickly, and therefore often receive less testing than the original software. Installing patches, modifying configurations, and uninstalling software may change the system behavior such that it causes other programs to crash or otherwise fail.

+ Installing one patch might also inadvertently uninstall or disable another patch. If there is a dependency, there is the need to ensure that patches are installed in a certain sequence. Also, it is important to determine whether other patches are uninstalled when a particular patch is installed.

+ Testing should be performed on a selection of systems that accurately represent the configuration of the systems in deployment, since so many possible system configurations exist that the vendor cannot possibly test against all of them. Thus, the remediation may have unintended consequences only on one particular configuration. After the remediation is performed, check that all related software is operating correctly.

+ Before performing the remediation, and especially if there is a lack of time or resources to perform a test on the patch before employing it on a production system, the PVG may wish to learn what experiences others have had in installing or using the patch. For instance, others' experiences could indicate whether the patch or configuration adjustment corrects the vulnerability, opens an old vulnerability, creates a new vulnerability, degrades performance, or is incompatible with other required applications. It is important to remember that others'

---

[14] Federal agencies are required to use FIPS-approved algorithms and FIPS-validated cryptographic modules. SHA-1 is a FIPS-approved algorithm, but MD5 is not. Accordingly, agencies should use SHA-1 checksums from vendors instead of MD5 or other checksums whenever SHA-1 checksums are available.

[15] Organizations should use existing change management procedures when possible for testing patches and configuration modifications. Also, using images of standard configurations on test systems or within virtual machines on test systems can expedite the testing process.

[16] Examples include enabling default user accounts that had been disabled, resetting the passwords for default user accounts, and enabling services and functions that had been disabled.

experiences might vary due to environment-specific factors, implementation differences, and other reasons.

+ If one or more of the above problems applies, the PVG will need to consider whether the disadvantages outweigh the benefits of installing the patch. If the remediation is not critical, it may be better to wait until the vendor releases a newer patch that corrects the major issues (this is a common occurrence). Also, the ability to "undo" or uninstall a patch should be considered; however, even when this option is provided, the uninstall process does not always return the system to its previous state.

2.7 Deploying Vulnerability Remediations

Organizations should deploy vulnerability remediations to all systems that have the vulnerability, even for systems that are not at immediate risk of exploitation.[17] Vulnerability remediations should also be incorporated into the organization's standard builds and configurations for hosts. There are three primary methods of remediation that can be applied to an affected system: the installation of a software patch, the adjustment of a configuration setting, and the removal of the affected software.

+ **Security Patch Installation.** Applying a security patch (also called a "fix" or "hotfix") repairs the vulnerability, since patches contain code that modifies the software application to address and eliminate the problem. Patches downloaded from vendor Web sites are typically the most up-to-date and are likely free of malicious code.

+ **Configuration Adjustment.** Adjusting how an application or security control is configured can effectively block attack vectors[18] and reduce the threat of exploitation. Common configuration adjustments include disabling services and modifying privileges, as well as changing firewall rules and modifying router access controls. Settings of vulnerable software applications can be modified by adjusting file attributes or registry settings.

+ **Software Removal.** Removing or uninstalling the affected software or vulnerable service eliminates the vulnerability and any associated threat. This is a practical solution when an application is not needed on a system. Determining how the system is used, removing unnecessary software and services, and running only what is essential for the system's purpose is a recommended security practice.

The mitigation of vulnerabilities and threats may be as simple as modifying a configuration setting, or as involved as the installation of a completely new version of the software. No simple patch application methodology applies to all software and operating systems. Before performing the remediation, the administrator may want to conduct a full backup of the system to be patched. This will allow for a timely restoration of the system to previous state if the patch has an unintended or unexpected impact on the host.

Applying patches to multiple systems is a constant administrative challenge that may seem especially daunting when implementing patches on hundreds or thousands of servers and desktop systems. This task can be made less burdensome with the use of applications that automatically distribute updates to end-user computers. These enterprise patch management tools are included with network operating system software and distributed by third-party vendors. The capabilities of these tools vary greatly. Some of these tools focus on the distribution of patches, relying on the system administrator to identify a necessary patch and arrange for the tool to deliver and install the patch. Other tools actively search for necessary

---

[17] For example, if a system has a vulnerable service disabled, the service is not immediately exploitable, but it could be enabled inadvertently or intentionally at any time, which would cause the system to be vulnerable.
[18] Attack vectors are the paths by which an exploit can penetrate a computer.

patches and automatically notify the system administrator of the available ones; the administrator can then approve the tool's installation of the patches on the appropriate hosts. Enterprise management tools can vary greatly in their support of different operating systems and applications. Those that are bundled with an operating system tend to support the fewest operating systems and applications. Those from third-party vendors are generally compatible with the widest range of systems. Automated patch distribution tends to work best for organizations with a relatively homogenous environment and standardized configurations. Refer to Section 4.1 for further information on enterprise patching solutions.

Organizations need to apply patches manually for operating systems and applications that their enterprise patch management tools do not support. Also, many appliance-based devices cannot be updated by patch management tools, even if the appliances use operating systems and applications that the patch management tools support. This is because appliances often use customized limited-functionality versions of operating systems and applications, which are not intended for administrators to access directly. Because the appliances' customized operating systems and applications are based on the same code as the standard programs, they are typically susceptible to many of the same vulnerabilities. However, the appliances often cannot be patched as quickly as standard devices, because patches for appliances typically can be applied only through updates provided by the device's manufacturer. In many organizations, the level of effort needed to apply patches manually for appliances and for operating systems and applications not supported by patch management tools is substantial.

Regardless of whether remediation involves automated patching or manual updates, system administrators may believe that the disadvantages of a suggested remediation outweigh its benefits. They may not wish to install the patches or perform the configuration modifications at all. The reasons behind these decisions should be documented and communicated back to the PVG and then to the appropriate management for approval.

The risk of delaying remediation must be weighed carefully. Consider the following:

+ **Threat Level.** Does the organization or systems requiring remediation face numerous and/or significant threats? For example, public Web servers and most Federal government organizations may face high threat levels. In general, timely remediation is critical for these systems. In contrast, for an intranet site that is inaccessible from the Internet, remediation can often be delayed because such a site usually faces a lower threat level.

+ **Risk of Compromise.** What is the likelihood that a compromise will occur? If the vulnerability is easy to exploit, then remediation should be applied swiftly.

+ **Consequences of Compromise.** What are the consequences of compromise? If the system is critical or contains sensitive data, then the remediation should be performed immediately. This holds true even for noncritical systems if a successful exploitation would lead to an attacker gaining full control of the system.

Unfortunately, neither decision—to apply or not apply a remediation—is risk-free. The correct decision is not always clear. The PVG, system administrators, and management must work together to create a systematic process for evaluating risks and determining the appropriate decision within the context of their organization. NIST recommends integrating the remediation process with the existing configuration management procedures to secure IT devices without causing unintended damage.

2.8 Distributing Vulnerability and Remediation Information to Administrators

The primary way in which the PVG will distribute patches is through enterprise patch management software. However, it is sometimes necessary for the PVG to communicate remediations directly to local administrators. E-mail lists should provide an effective method for distributing information regarding the priority of vulnerabilities, particulars about corresponding patches, configuration modifications, and other details. However, to decrease the chance of a spoofed e-mail containing a Trojan horse patch, actual patches should be distributed from the PVG to administrators from an internal secured Web site (ideally patches are distributed using automated patching tools). Additional controls may be used to support the integrity of the patches and the e-mail lists themselves, such as using digital signatures. Several e-mail lists may be maintained for administrators that are responsible for various types of systems (e.g., UNIX administrators, Windows administrators). Alternative methods of patch and information distribution, such as on disk, should be considered if the network or the secured Web site is unstable or unusable.

2.9 Verifying Remediation

The PVG and system administrators should verify that they have remediated or mitigated vulnerabilities as intended. There are understandable benefits in confirming that the remediations have been conducted appropriately, possibly avoiding experiencing a security incident or unplanned downtime. This can be accomplished by several methods:[19]

+ Verify that the files or configuration settings the remediation was intended to correct have been changed as stated in the vendor's documentation

+ Scan the host with a vulnerability scanner that is capable of detecting known vulnerabilities

+ Verify whether the recommended patches were installed properly by reviewing patch logs

+ Employ exploit procedures or code and attempt to exploit the vulnerability (i.e., perform a penetration test).

Only an experienced administrator or security officer should perform exploit tests, since this involves launching actual attacks within a network or on a host. Generally, this type of testing should only be performed on non-production equipment and only for certain vulnerabilities. The tests should only be conducted by qualified personnel who are thoroughly aware of the risk.

The following sections provide more details on using vulnerability scanners, reviewing patch logs, and checking patch levels when computers attempt to join an organization's network.

2.9.1 Performing Vulnerability Scanning

Vulnerability scanners are commonly used in many organizations to identify vulnerabilities on their hosts and networks. A vulnerability scanner identifies not only hosts and open ports on those hosts, but also associated vulnerabilities.[20] A host's operating system and active applications are identified and then compared with a database of known vulnerabilities. Vulnerability scanners can be of two types:

+ Network scanners are used to map an organization's network and identify open ports, vulnerable software, and misconfigured services. They can be installed on a single system on the network and can quickly locate and test numerous hosts. Network scanners are generally ineffective at gathering accurate information on hosts using personal firewalls, unless the personal firewalls are configured to permit the network scanning activity.

---

[19] Organizations should consider having the PVG verify remediations on new servers before they are deployed to production, if the PVG has sufficient resources.

[20] Running vulnerability scanners frequently can be helpful in identifying new hosts on a network, as well as their vulnerabilities.

+ Host scanners must be installed on each host to be tested. These scanners are used primarily to identify specific host operating system and application misconfigurations and vulnerabilities. Host scanners have high detection granularity and usually require not only host (local) access but also a root or administrative account. Some host scanners offer the capability of repairing misconfigurations.

Vulnerability scanners vary widely in capability and performance. Some of them perform optimized searching and can scan a host or network much faster than other systems. Some of them provide detailed reports and information about the remediation of each discovered vulnerability, while others provide only the most basic information about which vulnerabilities were found.

Vulnerability scanners employ large databases of vulnerabilities to identify vulnerabilities associated with commonly used operating systems and applications. The vulnerability database must be updated frequently so that the scanners can identify the newest vulnerabilities. When a match is found, the scanner will alert the operator to a possible vulnerability. Most vulnerability scanners also generate reports to help system administrators fix the discovered vulnerabilities. Unfortunately, as described in Section 3.3.2, vulnerability scanners are not completely accurate; some vulnerabilities may be missed, and other vulnerabilities that do not exist may be identified. Organizations should consider using multiple vulnerability scanning products so that false positives generated by one scanner can be validated by another. See NIST SP 800-42, *Guidelines on Network Security Testing*, for detailed advice on the use of vulnerability scanners.[21]

Vulnerability scanners provide the following capabilities:

+ Identify active hosts on networks

+ Identify active and vulnerable services (ports) on hosts

+ Identify vulnerabilities associated with discovered operating systems and applications

+ Test compliance with host application usage/security policies.

Vulnerability scanners can help identify out-of-date software versions and applicable patches or system upgrades.[22] In addition, certain vulnerability scanners are able to automatically make corrections and fix certain discovered vulnerabilities.

2.9.2 Reviewing Patch Logs

Log files keep track of the history of a system. Patch logs can assist the PVG, as well as system administrators, with tracking and verifying installed patches. Using patch logs to monitor an organization's systems can help to achieve consistency and compliance with the remediation plan. Patch logs can provide the following capabilities:

+ Identify which patches are installed on a system, allowing easy confirmation that the appropriate set of patches is applied on the system

---

[21] NIST SP 800-42 is available at http://csrc.nist.gov/publications/nistpubs/800-42/NIST-SP800-42.pdf.

[22] Generally, host-based scanners are more effective at doing this than network-based scanners. Although scanners can be helpful at finding outdated software, scanners may identify deliberately deployed settings as vulnerabilities. The person assessing the vulnerability scanner reports needs to know how to interpret them and compare them to the organization's business requirements.

- Ensure that patches are applied in a consistent manner across the organization through a comparison of log files
- Verify that a patch has been installed properly
- Determine whether the patch or a subsequent update improperly removed or damaged a previous patch.

2.9.3 Checking Patch Levels

An organization might wish to verify the patch levels of hosts before allowing them to join its networks. This can be done through the use of separate virtual local area networks (VLAN) for unverified hosts. In most deployments, each host runs an agent that monitors various characteristics, such as OS and application patches and antivirus updates. When the host attempts to connect to the network, a network device such as a router requests information from the host's agent. If the host does not respond to the request or the response indicates that the host is not fully patched, the network device causes the host to be placed onto a separate VLAN. This allows the organizations to update the unpatched hosts while severely restricting what they can do. Once a host on the VLAN has been fully updated, it is moved automatically from the VLAN to the organization's regular network. The VLAN strategy can be particularly helpful for ensuring that mobile hosts are fully patched.

2.10 Vulnerability Remediation Training

Although the PVG will monitor for new patches and vulnerabilities found within the software listed in the organizational software inventory, local administrators may use software not listed in the inventory. This situation may result from a management decision that the PVG only has resources to focus on the more popular software packages. In this situation, it is essential that local administrators have some knowledge of how to identify new patches and vulnerabilities. By providing them with such knowledge, a second line of defense is created in the patching process. Local administrators should be trained by the PVG on the various vulnerability and patching resources described in Section 2.3.2. Organizations may choose to train their administrators with only a few tools that are known to be comprehensive.

In addition, all end users who will be expected to implement recommended remediations on their own systems should be educated about the organization's vulnerability management process. These end users should also be provided with instructions on installing patches and performing other types of remedial actions. This expectation most likely applies to the organization's remote workers.

2.11 Recommendations

Organizations need to create a comprehensive, documented, and accountable process for identifying and addressing vulnerabilities, patches, and threats within an organization. One possible approach is to have a formal, centralized patch and vulnerability group that supports the security efforts of local system administrators.

Specific recommendations for organizations implementing a patch and vulnerability management program are as follows:

1. Create an inventory of all information technology assets.
2. Create a patch and vulnerability group.
3. Continuously monitor for vulnerabilities, remediations, and threats.

4. Prioritize patch application and use phased deployments as appropriate.

5. Test patches before deployment.

6. Deploy enterprise-wide automated patching solutions.

7. Create a remediation database (this is often included within enterprise patch management tools).

8. Use automatically updating applications as appropriate.

9. Verify that vulnerabilities have been remediated.

10. Train applicable staff on vulnerability monitoring and remediation techniques.

3. Security Metrics for Patch and Vulnerability Management

This section discusses how to develop and implement a patch and vulnerability metrics program. Every organization should consistently measure the effectiveness of its patch and vulnerability management program and apply corrective actions as necessary. Without such a capability, even the best-designed security architectures can be susceptible to penetration or other forms of exploit.

3.1 Implementing Security Metrics with NIST SP 800-55

NIST SP 800-55, *Security Metrics Guide for Information Technology Systems*, describes a security metrics development and implementation process.[23] Implementing this process will help demonstrate the adequacy of in-place security controls, policies, and procedures. It also will help justify security control investments and can be used in identifying necessary corrective actions for deficient security controls. SP 800-55 provides a variety of example security metrics but does not explore in detail the issues surrounding metrics for patch and vulnerability measurement. This publication builds on the foundation of SP 800-55 by discussing different types of patch and vulnerability measurements and discussing issues with taking such measurements.

3.2 Metrics Development

This section discusses patch and vulnerability metrics development in the context of measuring characteristics per system. The word "system", in this context, refers to a set of information technology (IT) assets, processes, applications, and related IT resources that are under the same direct management and budgetary control; have the same function or mission objective; have essentially the same security needs; and reside in the same general operating environment. It does not necessarily refer to individual computers. This usage of the word "system" is defined within NIST SP 800-18.

3.2.1 Types of Patch and Vulnerability Metrics

There are three main categories of patch and vulnerability metrics: susceptibility to attack, mitigation response time, and cost. This section provides example metrics in each category.

3.2.1.1 Measuring a System's Susceptibility to Attack

An organization's susceptibility to attack can be approximated by several measurements. An organization can measure the number of patches needed, the number of vulnerabilities, and the number of network services running on a per system basis. These measurements should be taken individually for each computer within the system, and the results then aggregated to determine the system-wide result.

Both raw results and ratios (e.g., number of vulnerabilities per computer) are important. The raw results help reveal the overall risk a system faces because the more vulnerabilities, unapplied patches, and exposed network services that exist, the greater the chance that the system will be penetrated. Large systems consisting of many computers are thus inherently less secure than smaller similarly configured systems. This does not mean that the large systems are necessarily secured with less rigor than the smaller systems. To avoid such implications, ratios should be used when comparing the effectiveness of the security programs of multiple systems. Ratios (e.g., number of unapplied patches per computer) allow effective comparison between systems. Both raw results and ratios should be measured and published for each system, as appropriate, since they are both useful and serve different purposes.

---

[23] NIST SP 800-55 is available for download at http://csrc.nist.gov/publications/nistpubs/800-55/sp800-55.pdf.

The initial measurement approach should not take into account system security perimeter architectures (e.g., firewalls) that would prevent an attacker from directly accessing vulnerabilities on system computers. This is because the default position should be to secure all computers within a system even if the system is protected by a strong security perimeter. Doing so will help prevent insider attacks and help prevent successful external attackers from spreading their influence to all computers within a system.

Recognizing that most systems will not be fully secured, for a variety of reasons, the measurement should then be recalculated while factoring in a system's security perimeter architecture. This will give a meaningful measurement of a system's actual susceptibility to external attackers. For example, this second measurement would not count vulnerabilities, network services, or needed patches on a computer if they could not be exploited through the system's main firewall.

While the initial measurement of a system's susceptibility to attack should not take into account the system security perimeter architecture, it may be desirable to take into account an individual computer's security architecture. For example, vulnerabilities exploitable by network connections might not be counted if a computer's personal firewall would prevent such exploit attempts. This should be done cautiously because a change in a computer's security architecture could expose vulnerabilities to exploitation.

Number of Patches

Measuring the number of patches needed per system is natural for organizations that have deployed enterprise patch management tools, since these tools automatically provide such data. The number of patches needed is of some value in approximating an organization's susceptibility to attack, but its effectiveness is limited because a particular security patch may fix one or many vulnerabilities, and these vulnerabilities may be of varying levels of severity. In addition, there are often vulnerabilities published for which there are no patches. Such vulnerabilities intensify the risk to organizations, yet are not captured by measuring the number of patches needed. The quality of this measurement can be improved by factoring in the number of patches rated critical by the issuing vendor and comparing the number of critical and non-critical patches.

Number of Vulnerabilities

Measuring the number of vulnerabilities that exist per system is a better measure of an organization's susceptibility to attack, but still is far from perfect. Organizations that employ vulnerability scanning tools are most likely to employ this metric, since such tools usually output the needed statistics.[24] As with measuring patches, organizations should take into account the severity ratings of the vulnerabilities, and the measurement should output the number of vulnerabilities at each severity level (or range of severity levels). Vulnerability databases (such as the National Vulnerability Database, http://nvd.nist.gov/), vulnerability scanning tools, and the patch vendors themselves usually provide rating systems for vulnerabilities; however, currently there is no standardized rating system. Such rating systems only approximate the impact of a vulnerability on a stereotypical generic organization. The true impact of a vulnerability can only be determined by looking at each vulnerability in the context of an organization's unique security infrastructure and architecture. In addition, the impact of a vulnerability on a system depends on the network location of the system (i.e., when the system is accessible from the Internet, vulnerabilities are usually more serious).

Number of Network Services

---

[24] As mentioned in Sections 2.9.1 and 3.3.2, vulnerability scanners are not completely accurate; they may report some vulnerabilities that do not exist and fail to report some that do exist.

The last example of an attack susceptibility metric is measuring the number of network services running per system.[25] The concept behind this metric is that each network service represents a potential set of vulnerabilities, and thus there is an enhanced security risk when systems run additional network services. When taken on a large system, the measurement can indicate a system's susceptibility to network attacks (both current and future). It is also useful to compare the number of network services running between multiple systems to identify systems that are doing a better job at minimizing their network services. Having a large number of network services active is not necessarily indicative of system administrator mismanagement. However, such results should be scrutinized carefully to make sure that all unneeded network services have been turned off.

3.2.1.2 Mitigation Response Time

It is also important to measure how quickly an organization can identify, classify, and respond to a new vulnerability and mitigate the potential impact within the organization. Response time has become increasingly important, because the average time between a vulnerability announcement and an exploit being released has decreased dramatically in the last few years. There are three primary response time measurements that can be taken: vulnerability and patch identification, patch application, and emergency security configuration changes.

Response Time for Vulnerability and Patch Identification

This metric measures how long it takes the PVG to learn about a new vulnerability or patch. Timing should begin from the moment the vulnerability or patch is publicly announced. This measurement should be taken on a sampling of different patches and vulnerabilities and should include all of the different resources the PVG uses to gather information.

Response Time for Patch Application

This metric measures how long it takes to apply a patch to all relevant IT devices within the system. Timing should begin from the moment the PVG becomes aware of a patch. This measurement should be taken on patches where it is relatively easy for the PVG to verify patch installation. This measurement should include the individual and aggregate time spent for the following activities:

+ PVG analysis of patch
+ Patch testing
+ Configuration management process
+ Patch deployment effort.

Verification can be done through the use of enterprise patch management tools or through vulnerability scanning (both host and network-based).

It may be useful to take this measurement on both critical and non-critical security patches, since a different process is usually used by organizations in both cases, and the timing will likely be different.

Response Time for Emergency Configuration Changes

---

[25] Organizations should consider assigning weights to services or network ports when counting them, because they may not all be equally important. For example, a single network port could be used by multiple services. Also, one service might be much more likely to be attacked than another or might perform much more important functions than another.

This metric applies in situations where a vulnerability exists that must be mitigated but where there is no patch. In such cases the organization is forced to make emergency configuration changes that may reduce functionality to protect the organization from exploitation of the vulnerability. Such changes are often done at the firewall, e-mail server, Web server, central file server, or servers in the DMZ. The changes may include turning off or filtering certain e-mail attachments, e-mail subjects, network ports, and server applications. The metric should measure the time it takes from the moment the PVG learns about the vulnerability to the moment that an acceptable workaround has been applied and verified. Because many vulnerabilities will not warrant emergency configuration changes, this metric will be for a subset of the total number vulnerabilities for any system.

These activities are normally done on an emergency basis, so obtaining a reasonable measurement sample size may be difficult. However, given the importance of these activities, these emergency processes should be tested, and the timing metric can be taken on these test cases. The following list contains examples of emergency processes that can be timed:

+ Firewall or router configuration change

+ Network disconnection

+ Intrusion prevention device activation or reconfiguration

+ E-mail filtering rules addition

+ Computer isolation

+ Emergency notification of staff.

The metric results are likely to vary widely between systems, since the emergency processes being tested may be very different. As much as possible, organizations should create standard system emergency processes, which will help make the testing results more uniform. Organizations should capture and review the metrics following any emergency configuration change as a part of an operational debriefing to determine subsequent actions and areas for improvement in the emergency change process.

3.2.1.3 Cost

Measuring the cost of patch and vulnerability management is difficult because the actions are often split between many different personnel and groups. In the simplest case, there will be a dedicated centralized PVG that deploys patches and security configurations directly. However, most organizations will have the patch and vulnerability functions split between multiple groups and allocated to a variety of full-time and part-time personnel. There are four main cost measurements that should be taken: the PVG, system administrator support, enterprise patch and vulnerability management tools, and incidents that occurred due to failures in the patch and vulnerability management program.

Cost of the Patch and Vulnerability Group

This measurement is fairly easy to obtain since the PVG personnel are easily identifiable and the percentage of each person's time dedicated to PVG support should be well-documented. When justifying the cost of the PVG to management, it will be useful to estimate the amount of system administrator labor that has been saved by centralizing certain functions within the PVG. Some organizations outsource significant parts of their PVG, and the cost of this outsourcing should be included within the metric.

Cost of System Administrator Support

This measurement is always difficult to take with accuracy but is important nonetheless. The main problem is that, historically, system administrators have not been asked to calculate the amount of time they spend on security, much less on security patch and vulnerability management. As organizations improve in their overall efforts to measure the real cost of IT security, measuring the cost of patch and vulnerability measurement with respect to system administrator time will become easier.

Cost of Enterprise Patch and Vulnerability Management Tools

This measurement includes patching tools, vulnerability scanning tools, vulnerability Web portals, vulnerability databases, and log analysis tools (used for verifying patches). It should not include intrusion detection, intrusion prevention, and log analysis tools (used for intrusion detection). Organizations should first calculate the purchase price and annual maintenance cost for each software package. Organizations should then calculate an estimated annual cost that includes software purchases and annual maintenance. To create this metric, the organization should add the annual maintenance cost to the purchase price of each software package divided by the life expectancy (in years) of that software. If the software will be regularly upgraded, the upgrade price should be used instead of the purchase price.

> Estimated annual cost = Sum of annual maintenance for each product + Sum of (purchase price or upgrade price / life expectancy in years) for each product

For example, an organization has the following software:

Product	Purchase price	Upgrade price	Life expectancy	Annual maintenance
Enterprise patch management software	$30,000	$15,000	4 years	$3,000
Vulnerability scanner	$20,000	$10,000	3 years	$2,000

Assume that the organization plans to upgrade the vulnerability scanner software after three years, but plans to switch to new enterprise patch management software after four years. The estimated annual cost will be ($3,000 + $2,000) + ($30,000/4) + ($10,000/3) = $15,833.

Cost of Program Failures

This measurement calculates the total cost of the business impact of all incidents that could have been prevented if the patch and vulnerability mitigation program had been more effective, as well as all problems caused by the patching process itself, such as a patch inadvertently breaking an application. The cost numbers should include tangible losses (e.g., worker time and destroyed data) as well as intangibles (e.g., placing a value on an organization's reputation). It should be calculated on an annual basis. The results of this measurement should be used to help evaluate the cost effectiveness of the patch and vulnerability management program. If the cost of program failures is extremely high, then the organization may be able to save money by investing more resources in their patch and vulnerability management program. If the cost of program failures is extremely low, then the organization can maintain the existing level of support for patch and vulnerability management or possibly even decrease it slightly to optimize cost effectiveness.

3.2.2 Targeting Metrics Towards Program Maturity

The emphasis on patch and vulnerability metrics being taken for a system or IT security program should reflect the patch and vulnerability management maturity level. A program with a low maturity level is likely to have a system with high susceptibility to attack, and metrics such as the vulnerability ratio should be of highest priority. More mature programs regularly fix all vulnerabilities, so attack susceptibility metrics are less useful. Such programs should focus on metrics related to their response time to emerging threats and vulnerabilities. Very mature programs should focus on optimizing their costs. While it is true that all metrics are important for programs at all maturity levels, this discussion is intended to prioritize the implementation of metrics.

NIST SP 800-26, *Security Self-Assessment Guide for Information Technology Systems*, defines maturity levels for various aspects of an IT security program:[26]

+ Level 1—control objective documented in a security policy

+ Level 2—security controls documented as procedures

+ Level 3—procedures have been implemented

+ Level 4—procedures and security controls are tested and reviewed

+ Level 5—procedures and security controls are fully integrated into a comprehensive program.

At each level, it becomes easier and less expensive to calculate metrics, as illustrated in Figure 3-1.

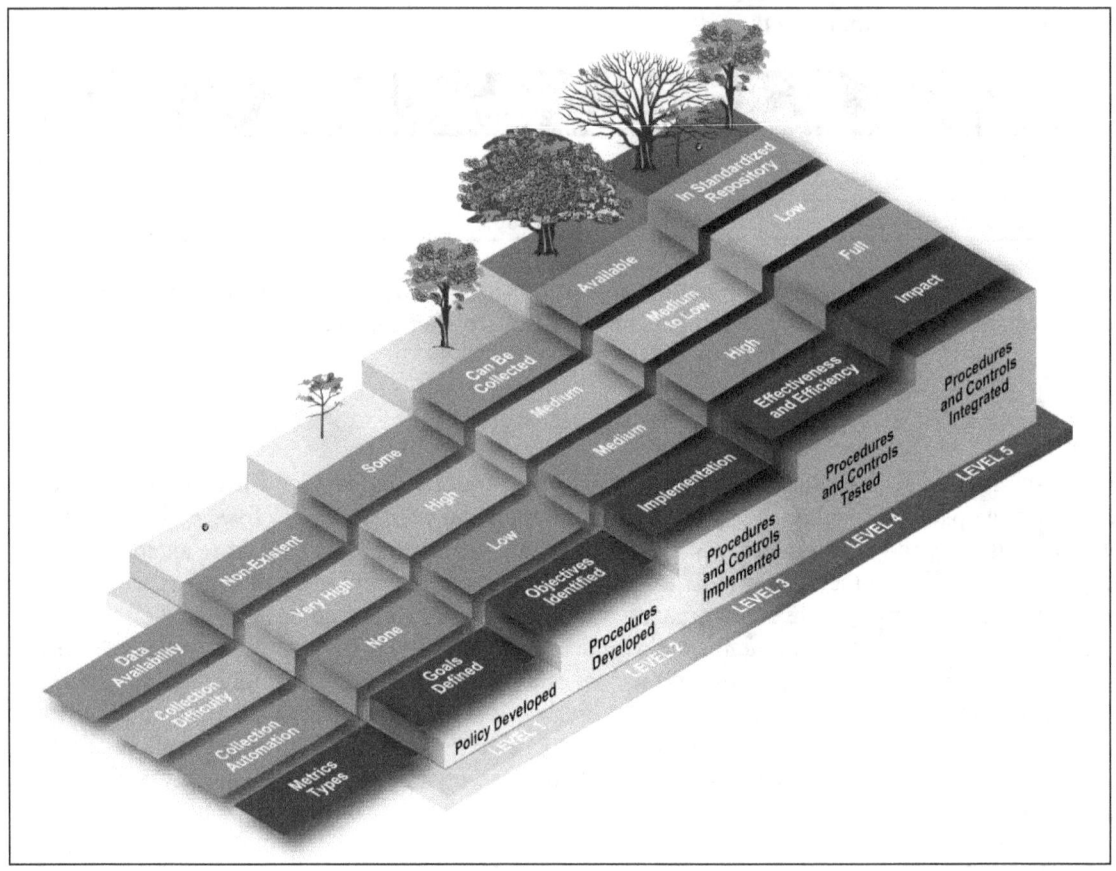

Figure 3-1. Maturity Levels for System Metrics

---

[26] NIST SP 800-26 is available at http://csrc.nist.gov/publications/nistpubs/. In August 2005, a draft of an updated version titled *Guide for Information Security Program Assessments and System Reporting Form* was released for public comment.

In the following section, these maturity levels are used to identify high-priority metrics for systems and programs at particular levels of maturity. Section 3.3 of NIST SP 800-55 provides more details on how metrics relate to program maturity.

3.2.3 Patch and Vulnerability Metrics Table

The following table summarizes the patch and vulnerability metrics. They should be taken on a per system basis, with the cost metrics a possible exception. It may be applicable to take them on a per organization basis if patch and vulnerability management is done at the organizational level.

Table 3-1. Patch and Vulnerability Metrics

Metric Name	Units	Targeted 800-26 Maturity Level
Vulnerability ratio	Vulnerabilities/Host	3
Unapplied patch ratio	Patches/Host	3
Network services ratio	Network Services/Host	3
Response time for vulnerability and patch identification	Time	4
Patch response time (critical)	Time	4
Patch response time (noncritical)	Time	4
Emergency configuration response time	Time	4
Cost of PVG	Money	5
Cost of system administration support	Money	5
Cost of software	Money	5
Cost of program failures	Money	5

3.2.4 Documenting and Standardizing Metrics

Organizations should document what metrics will be taken for each system and the details of each metric. NIST SP 800-55 provides a standard template for specifying security metric details.

3.2.5 Performance Targets and Cost Effectiveness

Realistic performance targets for each metric should be communicated to system owners and system security officers. Once these targets have been achieved, more ambitious targets can be set. It is important to carefully raise the bar on patch and vulnerability security to avoid overwhelming system security officers and system administrators.

The cost effectiveness of a program can be calculated by comparing the cost metrics associated with running the program to the cost of program failures. It can also be calculated by comparing the cost metrics associated with running the program to the metrics that indicate program performance (the response time and susceptibility to attack metrics).

3.3 Metrics Program Implementation

NIST SP 800-55 discusses how to implement a metrics program. This section augments that by providing information on certain patch and vulnerability metric implementation issues.

3.3.1 Starting From Scratch

Many organizations will start implementing metrics programs by using vulnerability scanning tools (both host and network-based) to measure the number of vulnerabilities per system. Initially, many organizations will turn on all of the vulnerability signatures within their scanning tools and then scan each system. The result is a useful measurement of the level of work needed to thoroughly secure all computers within each system. However, the vulnerability scanning output may be several hundred (or even a thousand) pages per system, and system security officers may become frustrated with handling such a large problem. Therefore, very little progress may be made.

A solution to this problem is to narrow the scan scope by prioritizing the vulnerability signatures and only scanning with the highest priority signatures. The system security officers can then focus on a more manageable problem and work to mitigate the most serious vulnerabilities. After a period of time, the list of vulnerability signatures that is used for scanning can be increased so that system security officers and administrators are consistently presented with manageable sets of work that will eventually lead to a more secure posture.

3.3.2 False Positives and False Negatives

All patch and vulnerability metrics programs will have to deal to some extent with false positives and false negatives. A false positive is when something (e.g., a vulnerability) does not actually exist but is counted in a measurement. A false negative is when something does exist but is not counted in a measurement. Historically, enterprise patch management tools have had few problems in this area; host-based vulnerability scanners have had more problems; and network-based vulnerability scanners have had the most problems.[27] However, enterprise patch management tools can encounter false positives even when they are working perfectly. For example, if a patch cannot be applied to a particular server, then the absence of the patch should not be counted in the metrics (although the server should be secured through alternate mechanisms). The PVG will have to keep track of known false positives and negatives and remove such issues from the measurement process.

Vulnerability scanners often include signatures that are intended for informational purposes. An "alert" on one of these signatures does not indicate an actual vulnerability. These informational signatures can be a large source of false positives within a vulnerability scanning program.

3.4 Recommendations

Every organization should consistently measure the effectiveness of its patch and vulnerability management program and apply corrective actions as necessary. This can be done by developing a patch and vulnerability metrics program. The metrics should be targeted toward the patch and vulnerability management program's maturity level, with particular metrics being most valuable for certain maturity levels. Organizations should document which metrics will be taken for each system and should document the details of each of the metrics. Realistic performance targets should be communicated to system owners and system security officers.

---

[27] Enterprise patching tools only look for the absence of patches, and thus have low error rates. Host-based scanners are often more error-prone because they look at more complex configuration information and vulnerabilities. Network-based scanners are often the most error-prone because they have access to only partial information about the scanned computers.

4. Patch and Vulnerability Management Issues

4.1 Enterprise Patching Solutions

All moderate to large-size organizations should be using enterprise patch management tools for the majority of their computers. Even small organizations should be migrating to some form of automated patching tool. Widespread manual patching of computers is becoming ineffective as the number of patches that need to be installed grows and as attackers continue to develop exploit code more rapidly. Only uniquely configured computers and other computers that cannot be updated effectively through automated means, such as many appliance-based devices, should continue to be patched manually.

4.1.1 Types of Patching Solutions

There are two primary categories of enterprise patch management tools: those that use agents and those that do not. Some products support both approaches and allow the administrator to choose the approach that is most efficient for the environment. With both approaches, there is usually a central computer that holds all of the patches that should be or could be installed on computers participating in the patching solution. The central computer will also often contain a console that allows the patching administrator to control which computers get which patches. Some implementations use multiple central computers to provide redundancy and divide the patching load across multiple devices and networks.

Both approaches utilize a centralized model with a single computer (or cluster of computers) controlling the patching process for all computers participating in the patching solution. This is in contrast to the standard Microsoft Windows Update service, which uses a completely decentralized model in which each computer (or the administrator of that computer) decides which patches to install and when to install them. Some products have features that combine the centralized and decentralized models. Such solutions usually follow the centralized model but give the end user some control over the process, such as the ability to choose not to install a patch.

While the two primary categories of enterprise patch management tools have similarities, they also have important differences that should be considered when purchasing a particular solution.

Non-Agent Patching Solutions

Non-agent patching solutions are similar to network-based vulnerability scanners. There is usually a single computer that scans computers through the network. However, unlike many vulnerability scanners, the non-agent patching solution is usually given administrator access to the computers participating in the automated patching program. This gives the patching program access to much more information than is available through simple network scanning. It also gives the patching program the ability to install patches on participating computers. Given the similarity between non-agent patching solutions and vulnerability scanners, it is not surprising that some commercial non-agent patching solutions also detect vulnerabilities, and can do so with greater accuracy than a vulnerability scanning program that does not have administrator access to the computer.

Since non-agent patching solutions rely on network scanning, they may consume a large amount of network bandwidth. Most products resolve this problem by enabling the patch administrator to throttle the amount of network bandwidth that is used by the product. However, limiting the network bandwidth that can be used by the product may increase the total amount of time needed to complete the network scan. In large networks, it may not be possible to scan all computers as quickly as needed, and agent-based solutions may be preferable. Additionally, computers for employees that telecommute might not be included in the scan. Another problem with non-agent patching solutions is that personal firewalls on computers will typically block the scanning activity unless they are specifically configured to permit it. Since the prevalence of personal firewalls is increasing, this is becoming a more significant problem.

Agent-Based Patching Solutions

Agent-based patching solutions, as mentioned previously, usually use a centralized computer (or cluster of computers) that manages the patching process for all participating computers. However, with this model a software program (agent) is installed on each participating computer.[28] While each product works differently, the overall agent patching process generally works as follows:

1. The agent communicates with the central computer to learn about new patches. Depending on the implementation, the agent may poll the central computer periodically or may be contacted directly by the central computer (which is more efficient).

2. The agent has administrator or root access to the computer, and it uses that privilege to determine which patches are missing. This status is usually transmitted to the central computer so that the overall patching administrator (e.g., PVG representative) can view the status of all participating computers. This also enables the central administrator to produce patching reports regarding the patch security level for each system.

3. The agent receives instructions from the central computer on which patches to install and how to install them. In cases where a reboot is required, the central computer may instruct the agent to patch and automatically reboot the computer. Alternately, the central computer may instruct the agent to patch and then notify the user that the computer needs rebooting (with the option of an automated reboot within a specified timeframe).

The architecture of the agent-based solution eliminates the excessive network bandwidth usage that may occur with the non-agent-based solution. The primary drawback is that the agents must be installed on each computer and must run with administrator or root privileges. Second, computers already taxed (running with high processing or memory loads) may suffer further performance degradation due to the agent process. Another possible drawback is that agents may not be available for all platforms, but platform support can also be an issue with non-agent approaches.

Advantages and Disadvantages of Each Approach

Each approach has advantages and disadvantages that should be considered.

Non-Agent Solution Advantages:

+ Does not need to install software agents on all participating computers.

Non-Agent Solution Disadvantages:

+ Utilizes a significant amount of network bandwidth while scanning computers.[29]

+ May require the use of ports and services that would otherwise be turned off as part of locking down the system (e.g., Remote Procedure Call [RPC] for UNIX, NetBIOS for Windows)

---

[28] As discussed in Section 2.7, many appliance-based devices do not permit direct administrator access to the operating system, which typically prevents the installation of patching agents.

[29] Both non-agent and agent solutions are likely to use approximately the same bandwidth for delivering patches to computers.

- May take a long time to scan large networks
- May not produce accurate results for hosts that use personal firewalls.
- May require that the central computer be given administrator access to participating computers.[30]

Agent-Based Solution Advantages:

- Can scan large networks quickly
- Minimizes use of network bandwidth while scanning computers.

Agent-Based Solution Disadvantages:

- Requires that software agents be installed, running, and managed on all participating computers. If an agent is not running due to failure or misconfiguration, the computer will not be patched.
- Must run agents with administrator or root privileges, which creates the possibility of remote attacks against agents that give attackers administrator privileges.

4.1.2 Security Risks

Deploying enterprise patch management tools within an enterprise can create additional security risks for an organization.[31] Despite this, such tools usually increase security far more than they decrease security, especially when the tools contain built-in security measures to protect against security risks and threats. The following are some risks with using these tools:

- A software vendor might distribute a patch to the enterprise patch management vendor that was corrupted with malicious code.
- The enterprise patch management vendor may provide a patch that has been maliciously altered by an employee or attacker.
- An attacker could break into the central patch computer and use the enterprise patch management tool as an efficient distribution tool for malicious code (potentially providing remote access to every participating computer).
- An attacker could break into the central patch computer on non-agent systems and steal the administrator passwords for all computers participating in the patch management program.
- An attacker could discover a locally exploitable vulnerability with the patch management agent software. This could enable the attacker to elevate access to a participating computer from user-level access to administrator access. This assumes that the attacker has already broken into the computer and gained access.
- An attacker could discover a remotely exploitable vulnerability with the patch management agent software. This could enable an attacker to remotely penetrate a participating computer and gain administrator access. It could also enable an attacker to launch a denial of service attack on the participating computer.

---

[30] Managing the credentials that the central computer needs to log on to the individual hosts can be very challenging if there are many individual accounts, particularly if passwords are changed very frequently (i.e., monthly).
[31] A much greater risk is faced by organizations that do not effectively patch their systems.

+ An attacker could sniff enterprise patch management tool network communications to determine which patches have not been installed on particular computers.

These risks can be partially mitigated through the application of standard security techniques that should be used when deploying any enterprise-wide application. Examples of countermeasures include the following:

+ Encrypting network connections
+ Performing IP address authentication for network communications
+ Disabling unneeded ports and services on the central patch management server
+ Testing patches before deployment
+ Performing timely application of patches
+ Conducting timely mitigation of vulnerabilities for which there are no patches
+ Using firewalls properly.

4.1.3 Integrated Software Inventory Capabilities

Enterprise patch management tools require administrator access to each participating computer and must inventory the software packages on each computer to determine which patches are needed. Therefore, it is natural for such programs to make this information available to the administrators and to incorporate a software inventory management capability within the product. An increasing number of products provide this capability, and it appears that this is the natural way for the market to move. Such inventory products can be purchased separately but often require a separate agent to be installed on each computer. Since it is costly from an IT management point of view to install and manage multiple agents on each computer, it would be ideal if both functions (patching and inventorying) could be performed by the same product.[32]

4.1.4 Integrated Vulnerability Scanning Capabilities

Enterprise patch management tools are also beginning to incorporate vulnerability scanning functionality. This enables the administrator to see not just which patches are missing, but also to understand what vulnerabilities are associated with those patches and thus understand what real risks exist to the unpatched computers. This capability also allows administrators to see vulnerabilities within computers before the patches are even available. This is very important, given the speed at which attack tools are developed whenever a new vulnerability is announced.

Not only do some of these tools have the capability to scan for vulnerabilities, but they may be able to scan for vulnerabilities with greater accuracy than network-based vulnerability scanners. Many network-based vulnerability scanners do not have administrator access to the computers that they scan, so they are forced to identify vulnerabilities by relying on imprecise guesses based on how different network ports respond to different inputs. Enterprise patch management tools do not have any such advantage over host-based vulnerability scanners. However, as with inventory management tools, it would be better to have patch management and vulnerability scanning capabilities integrated within one agent instead of having to install and manage two separate agents on each computer.

---

[32] Some patch management systems can only recognize software or versions of software that have known vulnerabilities. This would preclude the use of such a patch management system as the sole source of software inventory information for an organization.

4.1.5 Deployment Strategies

While all moderate to large-size organizations should be using enterprise patch management tools, deploying those tools universally within an organization can be difficult. It is recommended that organizations deploy enterprise patch management tools using a phased approach. This allows process and user communication issues to be addressed with a small group before deploying the patch application universally.

Most organizations deploy patch management tools first to standardized desktop systems and single-platform server farms of similarly configured servers. Once this has been accomplished, organizations should address the more difficult issue of integrating multiplatform environments, nonstandard desktop systems, legacy computers, and computers with unusual configurations. Manual methods may need to be used for operating systems and applications not supported by automated patching tools, as well as some computers with unusual configurations; examples include embedded systems, industrial control systems, medical devices, and experimental systems. For such computers, there should be a written and implemented procedure for the manual patching process.

While nonstandard systems and legacy computers can hamper a widespread deployment, personnel issues can be an even greater challenge. System owners (and computer users) may have some initial qualms about giving administrator access to their computers to another group and having that group regularly install and update software. Their concerns include the following issues:

+ The agent software may decrease computer performance or stability.

+ The patches being installed may cause unexpected problems with existing software.

+ A user may lose data when the enterprise patching application reboots the computer to install a patch.

+ The enterprise patching application may present a new security risk in and of itself.

+ A mobile user may become frustrated and confused when the enterprise patching application attempts to install a large set of patches as soon as the mobile user connects to the network.

These concerns should be discussed with system owners and computer users. All of them can be addressed by good communication, a careful phased rollout, and selection of a robust and secure enterprise patch management tool.

4.2 Reducing the Need to Patch Through Smart Purchasing

Some software products have more vulnerabilities than other products with equivalent purpose and functionality. By considering several factors during the purchasing process, organizations may be able to reduce the number of future vulnerabilities experienced and thus reduce the need to patch the software. The future likelihood of vulnerabilities should not be the only factor in purchasing a product, but it should be an element in the decision-making process. Another factor is the speed with which the vendor responds to new vulnerabilities with a patch. The following is a list of techniques for choosing products that are less likely to experience vulnerabilities in the future:

+ Consider a product for which there is a detailed checklist specifying how to secure the product. NIST manages the Security Configuration Checklists Program for IT Products, which collects reviewed checklists for a variety of operating systems and applications. NIST SP 800-70 describes the program, and it is available from the program's Web site, http://checklists.nist.gov/.

- Search a vulnerability database (such as the National Vulnerability Database at http://nvd.nist.gov/) for known vulnerabilities of products under consideration. Examine the type, severity, and quantity of vulnerabilities in the product under consideration. This is not foolproof because it often takes longer for vulnerabilities to be discovered (and patches released) for less popular software products.

- Consider a more mature product. Recently released products usually have more unknown vulnerabilities that will require future patches and possibly lead to increased exposure to risk.

- Consider less complicated products. More code, features, and services can mean more bugs, vulnerabilities, and patches. Consider not purchasing a product that has more features than needed. To the extent possible, delay implementing recently released major operating systems or applications until the experiences of others can be included in the decision-making process.

- Purchase products that conform to appropriate national or international security design standards (e.g., FIPS 140-2 for encryption modules). See NIST SP 800-23, *Guideline to Federal Organizations on Security Assurance and Acquisition/Use of Tested/Evaluated Products*, for more information.[33]

- Consider software validated by independent testing. For the greatest assurance, the software's source code should be evaluated.[34]

- Use only versions of software that are currently supported. Obsolete software beyond its lifecycle often has flaws that are only addressed in the newer, supported versions.

4.3 Using Standardized Configurations

Using standardized configurations for IT resources reduces the labor involved in identifying, testing, and applying patches, and ensures a higher level of consistency, which leads to improved security. Organizations that use standard configurations for their IT resources will find it much easier and less costly to implement a patch and vulnerability management program. Comprehensive patch and vulnerability management is almost impossible (or at least very costly) within large organizations that do not deploy standard configurations.

A standard configuration should be defined for each major group of IT resources (e.g., routers, user workstations, file servers). Organizations should focus standardization efforts on types of IT resources that make up a significant portion of their entire IT resources. Likely candidates for standardization include end user workstations, file servers, and network infrastructure components (e.g., routers, switches). The standard configuration will likely include the following items:

- Hardware type and model
- Operating system version and patch level
- Major installed applications (version and patch level)
- Security settings for the operating system and applications.

In many cases, these standardized configurations can be maintained centrally, and changes can be propagated to all participating IT resources. An organization that relies on a hardware supplier to place a standard configuration on new computers should coordinate closely with that supplier to ensure that

---

[33] NIST SP 800-23 is available for download at http://csrc.nist.gov/publications/nistpubs/800-23/sp800-23.pdf.
[34] Despite the benefit, software source code evaluations are generally not performed due to the cost of such an analysis.

changes, including new patches, are implemented quickly. NIST SP 800-70, *Security Configuration Checklists Program for IT Products—Guidance for Checklists Users and Developers*, provides guidance on creating and using security configuration checklists, which are helpful tools for documenting standard security settings.[35]

4.4 Patching After a Security Compromise

Patching after a security compromise is significantly more complicated than merely applying the appropriate patch. Although applying a patch after a security compromise will generally correct the vulnerability that was exploited, it will not eliminate rootkits, backdoors,[36] or most other changes that might have been introduced by the intruder. For example, the Code Red II worm placed backdoors on compromised systems, and later the Nimda worm exploited those backdoors. In most cases a compromised system should be reformatted and reinstalled[37] or restored from a known safe and trusted backup. If that is not possible, significant expertise will be required to manage the possible dangers inherent in compromised systems. NIST SP 800-61, *Computer Security Incident Handling Guide*, is an extensive resource for handling security incidents and recovering compromised computers.[38]

4.5 Recommendations

NIST recommends that moderate to large-size organizations use enterprise patch management tools for the majority of their computers. Small organizations should be migrating to some form of automated patching tool. Only uniquely configured computers and other computers that cannot be updated effectively through automated means, such as many appliance-based devices, should continue to be patched manually.

Deploying enterprise patch management tools can create additional security risks for an organization. For example, an attacker could break into the central patch computer and use the enterprise patch management tool as an efficient distribution tool for malicious code. Organizations should partially mitigate these risks through the application of standard security techniques that should be used when deploying any enterprise-wide application.

Organizations should deploy enterprise patch management tools using a phased approach. This allows process and user communication issues with a small group to be addressed before deploying the patch application universally. Most organizations deploy patch management tools first to standardized desktop systems and single-platform server farms of similarly configured servers. Once this has been accomplished, organizations should address the more difficult issue of integrating multiplatform environments, nonstandard desktop systems, legacy computers, and computers with unusual configurations. Manual methods may need to be used for operating systems and applications not supported by automated patching tools, as well as some computers with unusual configurations; examples include embedded systems, industrial control systems, medical devices, and experimental systems. For such computers, there should be a written and implemented procedure for the manual patching process. Concerns that system owners and computers users may have with giving administrator access to their computers to another group and having that group regularly install and update software should be addressed by good communication, a careful phased rollout, and selection of a robust and secure enterprise patch management tool.

---

[35] NIST SP 800-70 is available from the Security Configuration Checklists Web site at http://checklists.nist.gov/.
[36] A backdoor is a secret avenue of access placed on a compromised computer system by an attack that allows future unauthorized access.
[37] Organizations may find it helpful to maintain fully patched images of their standard configurations. A current, known good image can be placed onto a compromised system, then data restored from backups onto the system.
[38] NIST SP 800-61 is available at http://csrc.nist.gov/publications/nistpubs/800-61/sp800-61.pdf.

Some software products have more vulnerabilities than other products with equivalent purpose and functionality. By considering several factors during the purchasing process, organizations can reduce the number of future vulnerabilities experienced and thus reduce the need to patch the software. The future likelihood of vulnerabilities should be one element in the decision-making process. Another factor is the speed with which the vendor responds to new vulnerabilities with patches.

Another way that organizations can reduce the labor related to patch and vulnerability management is by using standardized configurations for IT resources. Organizations with standardized configurations will find it much easier and less costly to implement a patch and vulnerability management program. Comprehensive patch and vulnerability management is almost impossible within large organizations that do not deploy standard configurations. Organizations should focus standardization efforts on the types of IT resources that make up a significant portion of their entire IT resources.

5. United States Government Patching and Vulnerability Resources

In recent years, most of the United States government patch and vulnerability management products have been consolidated within the Department of Homeland Security's United States Computer Emergency Readiness Team (US-CERT). While US-CERT manages most of the products, NIST continues to produce publications and guidance in this area. This section discusses the US-CERT patch and vulnerability management products.

5.1 US-CERT National Cyber Alert System

The US-CERT National Cyber Alert System is a collection of three products: Cyber Security Alerts, Cyber Security Tips, and Cyber Security Bulletins.

+ **Cyber Security Alerts.** Cyber Security Alerts provide timely information about current security issues, vulnerabilities, and exploits. They outline the steps and actions that non-technical home and corporate computer users can take to protect themselves from attack. Cyber Security Alerts are available at http://www.us-cert.gov/cas/alerts/.

+ **Cyber Security Tips.** Cyber Security Tips describe and offer advice about common security issues for non-technical computer users. Tips are restricted to a single topic, although complex issues may span multiple tips. Each tip builds upon the knowledge, both terminology and content, of those published before it. Cyber Security Tips are available at http://www.us-cert.gov/cas/tips/.

+ **Cyber Security Bulletins.** Cyber Security Bulletins provide weekly summaries of security issues and new vulnerabilities. They also provide patches, workarounds, and other actions to help mitigate risk. Cyber Security Bulletins are available at http://www.us-cert.gov/cas/bulletins/.

5.2 Common Vulnerabilities and Exposures Standard

The Common Vulnerabilities and Exposures (CVE) vulnerability naming standard[39] is a dictionary of names for most publicly known IT vulnerabilities. This industry standard has achieved wide acceptance by the security industry and a number of government organizations. It is funded by US-CERT and the technical analysis work is done at MITRE Corporation. General CVE information is available at http://cve.mitre.org/. The vulnerabilities listed in CVE can be best viewed using the National Vulnerability Database, which is described in Section 5.3.

CVE provides the computer security community with the following:

+ A comprehensive list of publicly known vulnerabilities

+ An analysis of the authenticity of newly published vulnerabilities

+ A unique name to be used for each vulnerability.

NIST recommends using CVE-compatible vulnerability resources whenever possible. See http://cve.mitre.org/compatible/ for a list of CVE-compatible security products and services.

---

[39] CVE has not been adopted by any formal standards body. It is a widely used self-declared standard. NIST SP 800-51, *Use of the Common Vulnerabilities and Exposures (CVE) Vulnerability Naming Scheme*, is available at http://csrc.nist.gov/publications/nistpubs/800-51/sp800-51.pdf.

5.3 National Vulnerability Database

The National Vulnerability Database (NVD) is a vulnerability database that integrates all of the US-CERT vulnerability mitigation products, including the vulnerability notes described in Section 5.4 and the National Cyber Alert System products described in Section 5.1. It contains a fine-grained search engine that allows users to search for vulnerabilities containing a variety of characteristics. For example, users can search on product characteristics such as vendor name, product name, and version number, or on vulnerability characteristics such as severity, related exploited range, and type of vulnerability. NVD provides a vulnerability summary for each CVE vulnerability. Each summary contains attributes of the vulnerability (including a short summary and vulnerable version numbers) and links to advisories, patches, and other resources related to the vulnerability. NVD is built completely upon the CVE vulnerability naming standard and provides a searchable interface to the standard; NVD also supports queries in OVAL format, as described in Section 5.5. NVD was developed and is maintained by NIST in support of US-CERT's vulnerability mitigation product suite. NVD replaces the older ICAT vulnerability database product and is available at http://nvd.nist.gov/.

5.4 US-CERT Vulnerability Notes Database

The US-CERT Vulnerability Notes Database is a searchable database of short vulnerability advisories. These advisories, while significant, are not of sufficient importance and do not provide sufficient detail to be labeled as US-CERT Cyber Security Alerts. Users not specifically attempting to search US-CERT Vulnerability Notes may wish to search for vulnerabilities using NVD since it contains the US-CERT Vulnerability Notes as well as a variety of other vulnerability resources. The US-CERT Vulnerability Notes Database is available at http://www.kb.cert.org/vuls/.

5.5 Open Vulnerability Assessment Language

Open Vulnerability Assessment Language (OVAL) is a language for security experts to exchange technical details about how to check for the presence of vulnerabilities and configuration issues on computer systems. The vulnerabilities and configuration issues are identified using tests—OVAL definitions in Extensible Markup Language (XML)—that can be utilized by end users or implemented in information security products and services. OVAL is available at http://oval.mitre.org/.

5.6 Recommendations

NIST recommends that organizations take advantage of the publicly available vulnerability and patching resources provided by the U.S. government. These products should be directly used as a source of official and validated U.S. government information on vulnerabilities. Organizations should also use commercial products that provide interoperability with the U.S. government vulnerability and patching resources and standards.

There are several ways to use these resources. For example, organizations should consider purchasing vulnerability scanners that identify vulnerabilities using OVAL, list vulnerabilities using CVE names, and provide links to CVE vulnerability information in the National Vulnerability Database. Organizations should also subscribe to the US-CERT cyber security alerts to learn about the vulnerabilities that are considered most critical by the U.S. government, even if that organization subscribes to generic vulnerability services. This will help ensure that the highest priority vulnerabilities receive appropriate attention.

6. Conclusion and Summary of Major Recommendations

When designing a process for handling patches, consider the principles that make up the PVG patching concept. Other patching variations may be acceptable, but the core concepts should be found within the chosen patching methodology. These ideas include using organizational inventories, patch and vulnerability monitoring, patch prioritization techniques, organizational patch databases, patch testing, patch distribution, patch application verification, patch training, automated patch deployment, and automatic updating of applications.

Except for the smallest of organizations and select areas of large organizations, organizations should swiftly move to automated patching methods. The movement toward automated patch methods will parallel organizational plans to centralize services and standardize desktop configurations. For this reason, computer security personnel should be actively involved in designing centralized services and standardized desktop models.

While patching and vulnerability monitoring can often appear an overwhelming task, consistent mitigation of organizational vulnerabilities can be achieved through a tested and integrated patching process. Having a mature patch and vulnerability management program will make the organization more proactive than reactive with regard to maintaining appropriate levels of security for their systems. The efficiency of patch automation combined with preventative maintenance should result in spending less time, resources, and money on incident response. This document should aid those whose job it is to undertake this important and worthwhile task.

This publication contains a variety of recommendations to assist organizations in implementing an effective patch and vulnerability management program. A summary of the primary recommendations is as follows:

1. Create a patch and vulnerability group.

2. Continuously monitor for vulnerabilities, remediations, and threats.

3. Prioritize patch application and use phased deployments as appropriate.

4. Test patches prior to deployment.

5. Deploy enterprise-wide automated patching solutions.

6. Use automatically updating applications as appropriate.

7. Create an inventory of all information technology assets.

8. Use standardized configurations for IT resources as much as possible.

9. Verify that vulnerabilities have been remediated.

10. Consistently measure the effectiveness of the organization's patch and vulnerability management program, and apply corrective actions as necessary.

11. Train applicable staff on vulnerability monitoring and remediation techniques.

12. Periodically test the effectiveness of the organization's patch and vulnerability management program.

13. Use U.S. government vulnerability mitigation resources as appropriate.

Appendix A—Acronyms

Selected acronyms used in *Creating a Patch and Vulnerability Management Program* are defined below.

CVE	Common Vulnerabilities and Exposures
DMZ	Demilitarized Zone
DoS	Denial of Service
FIPS	Federal Information Processing Standard
FISMA	Federal Information Security Management Act
IP	Internet Protocol
IT	Information Technology
ITL	Information Technology Laboratory
NIST	National Institute of Standards and Technology
NVD	National Vulnerability Database
OMB	Office of Management and Budget
OVAL	Open Vulnerability Assessment Language
PDA	Personal Digital Assistant
PGP	Pretty Good Privacy
PVG	Patch and Vulnerability Group
RPC	Remote Procedure Call
URL	Uniform Resource Locator
US-CERT	United States Computer Emergency Readiness Team
XML	Extensible Markup Language

Appendix B—Glossary

Selected terms used in *Creating a Patch and Vulnerability Management Program* are defined below.

Application: Any data entry, update, query, or report program that processes data for the user.

Accreditation: The process by which certification is reviewed, and formal declaration made that a system is approved to operate and interconnect at an acceptable level of risk.

Administrative Access: An advanced level of access to a computer or application that includes the ability to perform significant configuration changes to the computer's operating system. Also referred to as "privileged access" or "root access".

Availability: Assurance that IT resources remain readily accessible to authorized users.

Backup: A copy of a system's data or applications that can be used if data is lost or corrupted.

Certification: The comprehensive evaluation of the technical and non-technical security features of a system, made in support of the accreditation process, that establishes the extent to which a particular design and implementation meet a specified set of security requirements.

Confidentiality: Assurance that information is not disclosed to unauthorized entities or processes.

Configuration Adjustment: The act of changing an application's setup. Common configuration adjustments include disabling services, modifying privileges, and changing firewall rules.

Configuration Modification: See "Configuration adjustment".

Exploit Code: A program that allows attackers to automatically break into a system.

Firewall: A program that protects a computer or network from other networks by limiting and monitoring network communication.

Host: A computer or IT device (e.g., router, switch, gateway, firewall). Host is synonymous with the less formal definition of system.

Hotfix: Microsoft's term for a security patch.

Integrity: Assurance that information retains its intended level of accuracy.

Misconfiguration: A configuration error that may result in a security weakness in a system.

Operating System: The master control program that runs a computer.

Patch: An additional piece of code developed to address a problem in an existing piece of software.

Remediation: The act of correcting a vulnerability or eliminating a threat. Three possible types of remediation are installing a patch, adjusting configuration settings, and uninstalling a software application.

Remediation Plan: A plan to perform the remediation of one or more threats or vulnerabilities facing an organization's systems. The plan typically includes options to remove threats and vulnerabilities and priorities for performing the remediation.

Risk: The probability that a particular threat will exploit a particular vulnerability.

Security Plan: Document that details the security controls (management, technical, and operational) established and planned for a particular formally defined system.

System: A set of IT assets, processes, applications, and related resources that are under the same direct management and budgetary control; have the same function or mission objective; have essentially the same security needs; and reside in the same general operating environment. When not used in this formal sense, the term is synonymous with the term "host". The context surrounding this word should make the definition clear or else should specify which definition is being used.

System Administrator: A person who manages the technical aspects of a system.

System Owner: Individual with managerial, operational, technical, and often budgetary responsibility for all aspects of an information technology system.

Threat: Any circumstance or event, deliberate or unintentional, with the potential for causing harm to a system.

Virus: A program designed with malicious intent that has the ability to spread to multiple computers or programs. Most viruses have a trigger mechanism that defines the conditions under which it will spread and deliver a malicious payload of some type.

Vulnerability: A flaw in the design or configuration of software that has security implications. A variety of organizations maintain publicly accessible databases of vulnerabilities.

Workaround: A configuration change to a software package or other information technology resource that mitigates the threat posed by a particular vulnerability. The workaround usually does not fix the underlying problem (unlike a patch) and often limits functionality within the IT resource.

Worm: A type of malicious code particular to networked computers. It is a self-replicating program that works its way through a computer network exploiting vulnerable hosts, replicating and causing whatever damage it was programmed to do.

Appendix C—Patch and Vulnerability Resource Types

This appendix discusses the advantages and disadvantages of the various types of resources that provide information on patches and vulnerabilities. The following resources are discussed:

+ Vendor Web sites and mailing lists
+ Third-party Web sites
+ Third-party mailing lists and newsgroups
+ Vulnerability scanners
+ Vulnerability databases
+ Enterprise patch management tools
+ Other notification tools.

C.1 Vendor Web Sites and Mailing Lists

Vendor Web sites are probably the most popular resource for information about new patches. These sites offer significant amounts of information and are the primary sources for downloading patches. Vendor Web sites offer several advantages:

+ Patches are released by the application vendors who developed and are most familiar with the product.
+ Patches downloaded from vendor Web sites are most likely free of malicious code.
+ Vendors often provide an array of information about vulnerabilities associated with their applications, including methods of mitigation and instructions for installing and using patches.
+ Vendors have unique expertise concerning their products.

Vendor Web sites do have some limitations:

+ Active notification may not be provided, so the site must be visited and reviewed frequently.
+ Numerous vendor Web sites may need to be monitored to encompass all supported products.
+ New vulnerabilities may not be listed in a timely manner, because many vendors will not report the vulnerability until the patch is available. The vulnerability and even exploit information may already have been posted on a third-party Web site or mailing list.

Many large vendors maintain mailing lists that enable them to send e-mail messages and notifications of vulnerabilities, patches, and updates to product users. These lists inform users of new vulnerabilities in a particular vendor's product line without having to regularly visit the vendor's security Web site. A drawback to these lists is that the PVG and system administrators may have to subscribe to numerous vendor lists to manage multiple operating systems or a large number of applications. In addition, vendors may use their mailing lists for marketing purposes, resulting in system administrators ignoring or filtering all messages from the list. Vendors do not generally distribute actual patches within e-mails since e-mail is not a secure delivery mechanism. If patches are distributed in e-mail, they should be digitally signed and the signature checked before being trusted.

C.2 Third-Party Web Sites

A third-party patch or vulnerability Web site is one that is not affiliated with an application vendor, and it may offer more detailed information than a vendor site. These Web sites may cover a large number of vendors and products or may specialize in a specific vendor or product. The Web sites often report new vulnerabilities before the vendor reports them because vendors often delay notification until they have confirmed the vulnerability and created a patch or other mitigation technique. Third-party Web sites offer several advantages:

- Timely release of information on new vulnerabilities
- Depending on the site:
    - Coverage of more than one vendor or product, allowing the system administrator to visit fewer Web sites to gather information (i.e., "one-stop shopping")
    - Specialization in a particular product or platform (saving the system administrators time because they do not have to navigate through unrelated data)
- For sites that allow site users to post:
    - Similar benefits as the third-party mailing lists and newsgroups (see Section C.3)
    - A filtering or rating mechanism that allows user to read only "high value" postings
- Potentially more acceptable alternatives to the official mitigation techniques provided by the vendor
- Information that the vendor chooses not to provide.

Third-party Web sites have some disadvantages:

- More likely for third-party patches to have unintended consequences or contain malicious code
- No comprehensive information on patching the vulnerability, requiring the research of multiple resources.

C.3 Third-Party Mailing Lists and Newsgroups

Mailing lists and newsgroups are threaded discussion groups that rely on e-mail. They are a way for users with similar interests to communicate with each other. The primary advantage of third-party mailing lists and newsgroups is that they allow system administrators and other users to interact in two-way communications, whereas vendor mailing lists support only one-way (vendor to user) communications. This allows system administrators to share their experiences and to ask questions. The principal difference between a newsgroup and mailing list is that a newsgroup is an "officially" recognized Internet forum and, as such, can only be established by following certain procedures. In contrast, anybody with a mail server and Internet access can set up a mailing list. Mailing lists may be moderated and participation controlled.

The advantages of third-party mailing lists and newsgroups are as follows:

- Allow interaction between system administrators
- Reduce the number of sites that a system administrator is required to search actively

- Allow a system administrator to learn directly from the experiences of others (e.g., are there problems associated with a particular patch, does it really correct the problem)
- May provide a workaround to be used until a patch is released.

The disadvantages of third-party mailing list and newsgroups are as follows:

- Generate a large number of e-mails that may not be useful to system administrators
- Potentially release sensitive information to unauthorized entities (a system administrator who asks questions relating to a system can inadvertently invite an attacker to try to exploit that vulnerability)
- Potentially increase exposure to malicious code because third-party fixes and workarounds are often created by unaccountable parties
- Expose an organization to unsolicited advertising (spam)
- Possibly provide inaccurate information
- May provide links to self-testing sites that automatically launch an exploit against hosts that visit the site (this may cause problems if an unpatched system visits the site).

C.4 Vulnerability Scanners

Vulnerability scanners are commonly used in many organizations to identify vulnerabilities on their hosts and networks. Vulnerability scanners employ large databases of vulnerabilities to identify vulnerabilities associated with commonly used operating systems and applications. There are two types of vulnerability scanners: network scanners and host scanners. Network scanners are used for identifying open ports, vulnerable software, and misconfigured services. Host scanners are used for identifying specific operating system and application misconfigurations and vulnerabilities. Refer to Section 2.9.1 for more information about vulnerability scanners.

Vulnerability scanners can:

- Proactively identify vulnerabilities
- Provide a fast and easy way to measure exposure
- Automatically fix discovered vulnerabilities
- Identify out-of-date software versions
- Validate compliance with an organizational security policy
- Generate alerts and reports about identified vulnerabilities.

However, vulnerability scanners do have some weaknesses. Scanners:

- Depend on regular updating of the vulnerability database
- Tend to have a high false positive error rate
- May generate significant amounts of network traffic

+ May cause a denial of service (DoS) of hosts, because scanner probing may cause a system to crash inadvertently.

C.5 Vulnerability Databases

Vulnerability databases are collections of searchable information on vulnerabilities that affect information systems. Many of these databases are publicly accessible via the Web. These Web sites are generally run by third parties not affiliated with software vendors, and can provide a wealth of information to system administrators and security professionals. They strive to cover most operating systems and software applications. Because they are not affiliated with software vendors, they often provide information that the vendor, or other organizations affiliated with the vendor, does not provide.

Vulnerability databases tend to be the quickest to report new vulnerabilities, which is both a benefit and a disadvantage. The provision of timely information on vulnerabilities can be critical to the success of a system administrator in securing a network.

Although the quantity and quality of information vary to some degree from site to site, vulnerability databases typically include the following types of information:

+ **Vulnerability Overview**—An introduction to the vulnerability that includes the CVE name; type of vulnerability; date the vulnerability was first publicly identified; date the vulnerability or patch information was last updated; and the operating system, application, or hardware affected by the vulnerability.

+ **Discussion or Analysis**—Detailed information on the vulnerability, from one paragraph to several pages, depending on the complexity of the vulnerability. This discussion may be highly technical.

+ **Solution**—A detailed discussion on mitigating or eliminating the vulnerability. Generally contains hyperlinks to the pertinent vendor's Web site for patches and updates. If available, other remediation techniques will typically be included.

+ **Exploit**—Information on exploiting the vulnerability and any applicable code, or links to other sites that have more information and exploit code. This information can be useful to the system administrator in determining whether a system is susceptible to exploitation (before or after the patch is applied). However, great care should be exercised in using these techniques so as not to cause unintended harm to systems.

Overall, vulnerability databases are one of the most powerful resources available. Even if other sources are principally relied upon for vulnerability information, the general news and discussions provided on the vulnerability database sites can prove invaluable.

C.6 Enterprise Patch Management Tools

The number of vulnerabilities and corresponding patches continues to grow, making manual patching of computers more difficult and less effective. Therefore, the majority of an organization's systems should participate in an enterprise patch management program. Enterprise patch management tools scan for vulnerabilities on computers participating in this patching solution, provide information regarding needed patches and other software updates on those computers, and allow an administrator to decide on the patching process.

There are two primary categories of enterprise patch management tools, those with agents and those that are agent-less. Both approaches typically involve a central computer that stores the patches that should or could be installed, as well as a console for the patching administrator to control the process. Each approach has advantages and disadvantages that should be considered. The primary advantage of agent-less patch management tools is that there is no need to install software agents on the computers involved in the patching solution. However, agent-less tools can consume significant amounts of network bandwidth and may take a greater amount of time to scan larger networks. Agent-based solutions scan larger networks more quickly and use a minimal amount of network bandwidth, but require the installation and management of software agents on each participating system. Section 4.1 provides detailed information about enterprise patching solutions.

Automated patch management tools and utilities are available from various vendors to assist in the identification of known vulnerabilities and automate the patch and vulnerability management process. The guidance provided in this document is an adjunct, not a substitute, for the documentation and recommendations of the product vendors.

C.7 Other Notification Tools

Because the task of keeping up with reports of vulnerabilities, releases of patches, and publishing of exploits has become more burdensome, various tools and applications have been created to provide the PVG and system administrators with automated and customized notifications for the systems they support. These tools are provided by vendors and third parties. Some products are free, while others require a one-time fee or subscription.

The advantages of these notification tools are as follows:

+ Customized notification limited to those applications and operating systems of interest

+ Real-time alerts to the system administrator (e.g., not requiring them to visit a Web page).

The disadvantages of these notification tools are as follows:

+ Cost (for fee-based services)

+ Information quality (these sources are only as good as the underlying information database)

+ Lag time inherent in certain services

+ Somewhat invasive, since an administrator must tell a third party which operating systems and applications are in use.

Appendix D—Patch and Vulnerability Resources

The lists below provide examples of resources such as software and Web sites that may be helpful in identifying known vulnerabilities and locating, acquiring, and applying patches for common operating systems and applications.

Common Patch Management Software

Software Name	Vendor	URL
Altiris Patch Management Solution	Altiris	http://www.altiris.com/products/patchmanagement/
ANSA	Autonomic Software, Inc.	http://www.autonomic-software.com/patch.html
BigFix Patch Manager	BigFix, Inc.	http://www.bigfix.com/products/products_patch.html
BindView Patch Management	Bindview Corporation	http://www.bindview.com/Solutions/VulnMgmt/ManagePatches.cfm
C5 Enterprise Vulnerability Management Suite	Secure Elements	http://www.secure-elements.com/products/
Ecora Patch Manager	Ecora Software	http://www.ecora.com/ecora/products/patchmanager.asp
eTrust Vulnerability Manager	Computer Associates International, Inc.	http://www3.ca.com/Solutions/Product.asp?ID=4707
GFI LANguard Network Security Scanner	GFI Software Ltd.	http://www.gfi.com/lannetscan/
Hercules	Citadel Security Software	http://www.citadel.com/hercules.asp
HFNetChkPro	Shavlik Technologies, LLC	http://www.shavlik.com/
HP OpenView Patch Manager using Radia	Hewlett-Packard Development Company	http://www.managementsoftware.hp.com/products/radia_patm/index.html
Kaseya Patch Management	Kaseya, Inc.	http://www.kaseya.com/prod1/pl/patch_management.phtml
LANDesk Patch Manager	LANDesk Software	http://www.landesk.com/Products/Patch/Index.aspx
LiveState Patch Manager	Symantec Corporation	http://sea.symantec.com/content/product.cfm?productid=30
ManageSoft Security Patch Management	ManageSoft Corporation Ltd.	http://www.managesoft.com/product/patchmanagement/index.xml
Marimba Patch Management	BMC Software, Inc.	http://www.marimba.com/products/solutions/patch-mgmt.html
NetIQ Vulnerability Manager	NetIQ Corporation	http://www.netiq.com/products/vsm/default.asp
Opsware Server Automation System	Opsware, Inc.	http://www.opsware.com/products/serverautomation/patchmgmt/
PatchLink Update	PatchLink Corporation	http://www.patchlink.com/products_services/patchlink_update.html
PolicyMaker Software Update	DesktopStandard Corporation	http://www.desktopstandard.com/PolicyMakerSoftwareUpdate.aspx
Prism Patch Manager	New Boundary Technologies	http://www.newboundary.com/products/prismpatch/prismpatch_info.htm
SecureCentral PatchQuest	AdventNet, Inc.	http://www.securecentral.com/products/patchquest/
Security Update Manager	ConfigureSoft	http://www.configuresoft.com/SUMMain.aspx

Software Name	Vendor	URL
Service Pack Manager	Gravity Storm Software	http://www.securitybastion.com/
Sitekeeper (Patchkeeper module)	Executive Software	http://www.execsoft.com/sitekeeper/sitekeeper.asp
Software Update Services	Microsoft Corporation	http://www.microsoft.com/windowsserversystem/updateservices/evaluation/previous/default.mspx
Systems Management Server	Microsoft Corporation	http://www.microsoft.com/smserver/default.asp
SysUpdate	SecurityProfiling Inc.	http://www.securityprofiling.com/eng/products/sysupdate.shtml
UpdateEXPERT	St. Bernard Software	http://www.patches-management.stbernard.com/
Windows Server Update Services	Microsoft Corporation	http://www.microsoft.com/windowsserversystem/updateservices/default.mspx
ZENworks Patch Management	Novell, Inc.	http://www.novell.com/products/zenworks/patchmanagement/index.html

Common Operating Systems

Web Site or Page Name	URL
Apple	
Apple Support	http://www.apple.com/support/
Apple Downloads	http://www.apple.com/support/downloads/
BSD	
FreeBSD Security Information	http://www.freebsd.org/security/index.html
Getting FreeBSD	http://www.freebsd.org/where.html
OpenBSD Security	http://www.openbsd.org/security.html
Getting OpenBSD	http://www.openbsd.org/ftp.html
Cisco	
Cisco Product Security Incident Response	http://www.cisco.com/en/US/products/products_security_vulnerability_policy.html
Improving Security on Cisco Routers	http://www.cisco.com/warp/public/707/21.html
Products & Services Security Advisories	http://www.cisco.com/en/US/products/products_security_advisories_listing.html
Technical Support & Documentation	http://www.cisco.com/en/US/support/index.html
Linux[40]	
Debian GNU/Linux Security Information	http://www.debian.org/security/
Getting Debian	http://www.debian.org/distrib/
Fedora Download	http://fedora.redhat.com/download/
How to Download [Fedora] Updates	http://fedora.redhat.com/download/updates.html
Mandriva Linux Download	http://www.mandrivalinux.com/en/ftp.php3
Mandriva Security Advisories	http://www.mandriva.com/security/
Ubuntu Linux Download	http://www.ubuntulinux.org/download/
Ubuntu Support	http://www.ubuntulinux.org/support/
Microsoft	

---

[40] This table lists some of the most popular Linux distributions of the hundreds available. For information on other distributions, see DistroWatch.com (http://distrowatch.com/).

Web Site or Page Name	URL
Microsoft Download Center	http://www.microsoft.com/downloads/search.aspx?displaylang=en
Microsoft Help and Support	http://support.microsoft.com/default.aspx
Microsoft Security Home Page	http://www.microsoft.com/security/default.mspx
Microsoft Security Notification Service	http://www.microsoft.com/technet/security/bulletin/notify.mspx
Microsoft Windows Update	http://windowsupdate.microsoft.com/
Security Bulletins	http://www.microsoft.com/security/bulletins/alerts.mspx
Novell	
Novell Security	http://www.novell.com/products/security.html
Novell Support	http://support.novell.com/
Sun	
Solaris Download	http://www.sun.com/software/solaris/get.jsp
Solaris Live Upgrade	http://www.sun.com/software/solaris/liveupgrade/
Sun Update Connection--Patches and Updates	http://sunsolve.sun.com/pub-cgi/show.pl?target=patchpage
SunSolve Online	http://sunsolve.sun.com/

Common Client Applications

Product Line	Vendor	URL
Compression Utilities		
7-Zip	7-Zip/Igor Pavlov	http://www.7-zip.org/download.html
ArchiveXpert	Concepts for Future	http://archivexpert.com/download/
PicoZip	Acubix	http://www.picozip.com/downloads.html
PKZip	PKWare	http://www.pkware.com/business_and_developers/support/updates/
PowerArchiver	ConeXware, Inc.	http://www.powerarchiver.com/download/
PowerZip	Trident Software Pty Ltd	http://www.powerzip.biz/download.aspx
SecureZip	PKWare	http://www.pkware.com/business_and_developers/support/updates/
StuffIt	Allume Systems Inc.	http://www.stuffit.com/
WinZip	WinZip Computing	http://www.winzip.com/downwzeval.htm
ZipMagic	Allume Systems Inc.	http://www.stuffit.com/win/zipmagic/
E-mail Clients		
Balsa	GNOME Project	http://balsa.gnome.org/download.html
Barca	Poco Systems, Inc.	http://www.pocosystems.com/home/index.php?option=content&task=category&sectionid=2&id=21&Itemid=38
Eudora	Qualcomm	http://www.eudora.com/download/
Eureka Email	Eureka Email	http://www.eureka-email.com/Download.html
GNUMail.app	Collaboration-world.com	http://www.collaboration-world.com/cgi-bin/project/release.cgi?pid=2
GyazMail	GyazSquare	http://www.gyazsquare.com/gyazmail/download.php
i.Scribe	Memecode Software	http://www.memecode.com/scribe.php
InScribe	Memecode Software	http://www.memecode.com/inscribe.php

Product Line	Vendor	URL
KMail	Kmail	http://kmail.kde.org/download.html
Mac OS X Mail	Apple	http://www.apple.com/support/panther/mail/
Mailsmith	Bare Bones Software	http://www.barebones.com/support/mailsmith/updates.shtml
Mercury Mail Transport System	David Harris	http://www.pmail.com/patches.htm
Mozilla	Mozilla	http://www.mozilla.org/security/
Mutt	Mutt	http://www.mutt.org/download.html
Nisus Email	Nisus Software	http://www.nisus.com/NisusEmail/FAQ.php?PHPSESSID=0ba9f9639672d1fdf836a97f3ad29383#HowUpgradeOS9
Outlook	Microsoft	http://office.microsoft.com/en-us/officeupdate/default.aspx
Outlook Express	Microsoft	http://www.microsoft.com/downloads/search.aspx?displaylang=en&categoryid=7
Pegasus Mail	David Harris	http://www.pmail.com/patches.htm
Pine	University of Washington	http://www.washington.edu/pine/getpine/
PocoMail	Poco Systems, Inc.	http://www.pocosystems.com/home/
Sylpheed	Sylpheed	http://sylpheed.good-day.net/
Thunderbird	Mozilla	http://www.mozilla.org/products/thunderbird/
VM	VM	http://www.wonderworks.com/vm/download.html
FTP Clients		
BulletProof FTP Client	BulletProof Software	http://www.bpftp.com/download.php
CuteFTP Professional	GlobalSCAPE	http://www.cuteftp.com/downloads/cuteftppro.asp
FileZilla	FileZilla	http://sourceforge.net/projects/filezilla/
FlashFXP	IniCom Networks	http://www.flashfxp.com/download.php
FTP Voyager	Rhino Software	http://www.ftpvoyager.com/dn.asp
gFTP	Brian Masney	http://gftp.seul.org/
NcFTP	NcFTP Software	http://www.ncftp.com/download/
SmartFTP	SmartFTP	http://www.smartftp.com/download/
Transmit 3	Panic, Inc.	http://www.panic.com/transmit/index.html
WS_FTP Professional	Ipswitch	http://www.ipswitch.com/support/WS_FTP/patch-upgrades.html
Instant Messaging Clients		
AOL Instant Messenger	AOL	http://www.aim.com/download.adp?aolp=1
GAIM	GAIM	http://gaim.sourceforge.net/downloads.php
Jabber	Jabber, Inc.	http://www.jabber.com/index.cgi?CONTENT_ID=503
Lumen Instant Messenger	Novell	http://www.novell.com/partnerguide/product/200671.html
Miranda	Miranda	http://sourceforge.net/project/showfiles.php?group_id=94142
MSN Messenger	Microsoft	http://messenger.msn.com/Download/
Trillian	Cerulean Studios	http://www.download.com/Trillian/3000-2150-10047473.html
Vypress Messenger	Vypress	http://www.vypress.com/products/messenger/

Product Line	Vendor	URL
Windows Messenger	Microsoft	http://www.microsoft.com/downloads/search.aspx?displaylang=en
Yahoo Messenger	Yahoo	http://messenger.yahoo.com/messenger/security/
Multimedia Utilities		
Flash	Macromedia	http://www.macromedia.com/downloads/
iTunes	Apple	http://www.apple.com/itunes/download/
QuickTime	Apple	http://www.apple.com/support/
Real Player	Real	http://service.real.com/realplayer/security/
Shockwave	Macromedia	http://www.macromedia.com/downloads/
Winamp	Winamp	http://www.winamp.com/player/free.php
Windows Media Player	Microsoft	http://www.microsoft.com/windows/windowsmedia/player/download/download.aspx
Office Productivity Tools		
Acrobat	Adobe	http://www.adobe.com/support/downloads/main.html
AppleWorks	Apple	http://www.apple.com/support/appleworks/
Microsoft Office	Microsoft	http://office.microsoft.com/en-us/officeupdate/default.aspx?displaylang=EN
Microsoft Works	Microsoft	http://www.microsoft.com/products/works/downloads.mspx
NeoOffice	NeoOffice	http://www.planamesa.com/neojava/en/download.php
OpenOffice	OpenOffice.org	http://www.openoffice.org/
StarOffice	Sun	http://www.sun.com/download/index.jsp?cat=Patches%20%26%20Updates&tab=3
WordPerfect Office	Corel	http://www.corel.com/servlet/Satellite?pagename=Corel3/Downloads/SupportDownloads
SSH Clients		
OpenSSH	OpenBSD Project	http://www.openssh.com/
PuTTY	Simon Tatham	http://www.chiark.greenend.org.uk/~sgtatham/putty/download.html
Reflection for Secure IT	AttachmateWRQ	http://download.wrq.com/
SecureCRT	VanDyke Software	http://www.vandyke.com/support/index.html
SSH Tectia	SSH Communications Security	http://www.ssh.com/support/downloads/
Web Browsers		
Camino	Mozilla	http://www.caminobrowser.org/
Firefox	Mozilla	http://www.mozilla.org/security/
Internet Explorer	Microsoft	http://www.microsoft.com/windows/ie/downloads/default.mspx
Konqueror	KDE	http://www.kde.org/download/
Mozilla Suite	Mozilla	http://www.mozilla.org/security/
Netscape	Netscape Communications	http://channels.netscape.com/ns/browsers/default.jsp
Opera	Opera Software	http://www.opera.com/download/
Safari	Apple	http://www.apple.com/support/downloads/safari.html

Common Server Applications

Product Name	Vendor	URL
Application Servers		
Apache Tomcat	Apache Foundation	http://jakarta.apache.org/site/downloads/downloads_tomcat.html
BEA Web Logic Server	BEA Systems	http://commerce.bea.com/index.jsp
Borland Enterprise Server	Borland	http://www.borland.com/downloads/download_bes.html
Flash Communication Server	Macromedia	http://www.macromedia.com/support/flashcom/downloads_updaters.html
HAHTsite	HAHT Commerce	http://www.haht.com/HAHTsite/
IBM WebSphere Application Server	IBM	http://www.ibm.com/products/finder/us/finders?pg=ddfinder
Interbase	Borland	http://www.borland.com/downloads/download_interbase.html
JBoss	JBoss	http://www.jboss.org/downloads/index
JRun Application Server	Macromedia	http://www.macromedia.com/support/jrun/updaters.html
Oracle Application Server	Oracle	http://www.oracle.com/technology/software/products/ias/index.html
Orion Application Server	Orion	http://www.orionserver.com/
Pramati Server	Pramati Technologies	http://www.pramati.com/index.jsp?id=downloads_archive&product=psv
Sun Java System Application Server	Sun	http://www.sun.com/download/index.jsp?cat=Patches%20%26%20Updates&tab=3
Zope	Zope Community	http://www.zope.org/Products/
Collaboration Servers		
GroupWise	Novell	http://support.novell.com/support_options.html
Lotus Domino	IBM	http://www-132.ibm.com/content/home/store_IBMPublicUSA/en_US/Upgrades.html
Novell Evolution	Novell	http://support.novell.com/support_options.html
SUSE Linux OpenExchange Server	Novell	http://www.novell.com/products/openexchange/download.html
TeamWare Office	TeamWare Group	http://www.teamware.net/Resource.phx/download/index.htx
WebBoard	Akiva	http://www.akiva.com/downloads/index.cfm?id=webboard
Windows SharePoint Services	Microsoft	http://www.microsoft.com/windowsserver2003/technologies/sharepoint/default.mspx
Database Servers		
DB2	IBM	https://www-927.ibm.com/search/SupportSearchWeb/SupportSearch?pageCode=SBD&brand=db2
Informix	IBM	http://www-306.ibm.com/software/data/informix/support/
Microsoft SQL Server	Microsoft	http://www.microsoft.com/sql/downloads/default.asp
MySQL	MySQL	http://dev.mysql.com/downloads/

Product Name	Vendor	URL
Oracle	Oracle	http://www.oracle.com/technology/software/index.html
Pervasive PSQL	Pervasive Software	http://www.pervasive.com/support/updates/?product=psql
PostgreSQL	PostgreSQL Global Development Group	http://www.postgresql.org/ftp/source/
DNS Servers		
BIND	Internet Systems Consortium	http://www.isc.org/index.pl?/sw/bind/
djbdns	D. J. Bernstein	http://cr.yp.to/djbdns/install.html
Microsoft DNS	Microsoft	http://www.microsoft.com/technet/prodtechnol/windowsserver2003/technologies/featured/dns/default.mspx
Nominum Foundation	Nominum	http://www.nominum.com/open_source_support.php?stype=2&sind=2
NSD	NLnet Labs	http://www.nlnetlabs.nl/nsd/index.html
PowerDNS	PowerDNS	http://www.powerdns.com/en/downloads.aspx
E-mail Servers		
602LAN Suite	Software602	http://support.software602.com/updates/
ArGoSoft Mail Server	ArGoSoft	http://www.argosoft.com/mailserver/download.aspx
CommuniGate Pro	Stalker Software	http://www.stalker.com/CommuniGatePro/
Eudora Internet Mail Server (EIMS)	Glenn Anderson	http://www.eudora.co.nz/updates.html
Eudora WorldMail Server	Qualcomm	http://www.eudora.com/download/worldmail/
Exim	Exim	http://www.exim.org/
IMail Server	Ipswitch	http://www.ipswitch.com/support/imail/releases/imail_professional/index.asp
inFusion Mail Server	CoolFusion	http://www.coolfusion.com/downloads/
Kaspersky SMTP Gateway for UNIX	Kaspersky	http://www.kaspersky.com/productupdates/
Kerio MailServer	Kerio Technologies	http://www.kerio.com/subscription.html
Lotus Domino	IBM	http://www-132.ibm.com/content/home/store_IBMPublicUSA/en_US/Upgrades.html
MailEnable	MailEnable	http://www.mailenable.com/hotfix/default.asp
MailMax	Smartmax Software	http://www.smartmax.com/mmupgradecenter.aspx
MailSite	Rockliffe	http://www.rockliffe.com/userroom/download.asp
MDaemon	alt-n Technologies	http://www.altn.com/download/default.asp?product_id=MDaemon
Merak Mail Server	Merak	http://www.merakmailserver.com/Download/
Microsoft Exchange	Microsoft	http://www.microsoft.com/exchange/downloads/2003/default.mspx
Postfix	Wietse Venema	http://www.postfix.org/download.html
Sendmail (commercial version)	Sendmail, Inc.	http://www.sendmail.com/support/download/patch_page.shtml
sendmail (freeware version)	Sendmail Consortium	http://www.sendmail.org/
Xmail	Davide Libenzi	http://www.xmailserver.org/

Product Name	Vendor	URL
FTP Servers		
ArGoSoft FTP Server	ArGoSoft	http://www.argosoft.com/ftpserver/upgrade.aspx
BulletProof FTP Server	BulletProof Software	http://www.bpftpserver.com/download.php
CrushFTP Server	CrushFTP	http://www.crushftp.com/download.html
GuildFTPd FTP Server Daemon	GuildFTPd	http://www.guildftpd.com/
RaidenFTPD	Raiden	http://www.raidenftpd.com/en/download.html
Rumpus FTP	Maxum Development Corporation	http://www.maxum.com/Rumpus/Upgrades.html
Secure FTP Server	GlobalSCAPE	http://www.cuteftp.com/gsftps/upgrade.asp
Serv-U FTP Server	Serv-U	https://rhinosoft.com/custsupport/index.asp?prod=rs
SurgeFTP	NetWin	http://netwinsite.com/cgi-bin/keycgi.exe?cmd=download&product=surgeftp
Titan FTP Server	South River Technologies	http://www.southrivertech.com/index.php?pg=./download/index&pgr=./purchase/index
Vermillion FTP Daemon	Arcane Software, Inc.	http://www.arcanesoft.com/
WS_FTP Server	Ipswitch	http://www.ipswitch.com/support/ws_ftp-server/patch-upgrades.asp
Web Servers		
4D WebSTAR	4D	http://www.4d.com/products/downloads_4dws.html
AOLserver	AOLserver	http://aolserver.sourceforge.net/
Apache HTTP Server	Apache Foundation	http://www.apache.org/dist/httpd/
Commerce Server/400	iNet	http://www.inetmi.com/iseries/commerce/ptf.html
Jigsaw	W3C	http://www.w3.org/Jigsaw/
Microsoft Internet Information Services	Microsoft	http://www.microsoft.com/technet/security/prodtech/IIS.mspx
RaidenHTTPD	Raiden	http://www.raidenhttpd.com/en/download.html
Roxen WebServer	Roxen Internet Software	http://download.roxen.com/4.0/
Sambar Server	Sambar Technologies	http://www.sambar.com/download.htm
SimpleServer:WWW	AnalogX	http://www.analogx.com/contents/download/network/sswww.htm
Sun Java System Web Server	Sun	http://sunsolve.sun.com/pub-cgi/show.pl?target=patchpage
Tcl Web Server	Tcl Developer Exchange	http://www.tcl.tk/software/tclhttpd/
Zeus Web Server	Zeus Technology	http://support.zeus.com/doc/zws/v4/supported_versions.html

Common Enterprise Firewalls

Product Line	Vendor	URL
BorderWare Firewall Server	BorderWare Technologies	http://www.borderware.com/support/
Cisco PIX	Cisco Systems	http://www.cisco.com/en/US/support/index.html
CyberGuard	CyberGuard Corporation	http://www.cyberguard.com/support/index.html?lang=de_EN
DX	Resilience Corporation	http://www.resilience.com/support/support.html
Firebox	WatchGuard Technologies, Inc.	http://www.watchguard.com/archive/service.asp
FireWall-1	Check Point Software Technologies	http://www.checkpoint.com/downloads/index.jsp
FortiGate	Fortinet	http://support.fortinet.com/
GB	Global Technology Associates	http://www.gta.com/support/upgrade/
Kerio Server Firewall	Kerio Technologies, Inc.	http://www.kerio.com/ksf_download.html
NetScreen	Juniper Networks, Inc.	http://www.juniper.net/customers/support/
Sidewinder	Secure Computing Corporation	http://www.securecomputing.com/index.cfm?skey=246
SonicWALL	SonicWALL	http://www.sonicwall.com/products/gav_ips_spyware.html
Sun Cobalt	Sun	http://sunsolve.sun.com/pub-cgi/show.pl?target=cobalt/index&nav=patchpage
Symantec Enterprise Firewall	Symantec Corporation	http://www.symantec.com/downloads/

Common Enterprise Network Intrusion Detection and Prevention Systems

Product Line	Vendor	URL
Attack Mitigator	Top Layer Networks	http://www.toplayer.com/content/support/index.jsp
Bro	Vern Paxson	http://bro-ids.org/download.html
Captus	Captus Networks	http://www.captusnetworks.com/info/support/index.html
Cisco IPS	Cisco Systems	http://www.cisco.com/en/US/support/index.html
Cyclops	e-Cop.net	http://www.e-cop.net/
DefensePro	Radware, Ltd.	http://www.radware.com/content/security/serviceinfo/default.asp
Dragon	Enterasys Networks, Inc.	https://dragon.enterasys.com/
eTrust Intrusion Detection	Computer Associates	http://www.my-etrust.com/Support/TechSupport.aspx
IntruShield	Network Associates	http://www.mcafee.com/us/downloads/default.asp
iPEnforcer	iPolicy Networks	http://www.ipolicynetworks.com/support/index.html
ManHunt	Symantec Corporation	http://www.symantec.com/techsupp/enterprise/select_product_updates_nojs.html
Mazu Enforcer	Mazu Networks, Inc.	https://supportcenteronline.com/ics/support/default.asp?deptID=735
NetDetector	Niksun	http://www.niksun.com/Support_Technical_Support.htm
Netscreen	Netscreen Technologies	http://www.juniper.net/customers/csc/software/

Product Line	Vendor	URL
Proventia	Internet Security Systems	http://www.iss.net/support/
SecureNet	Intrusion Inc.	https://serviceweb.intrusion.com/
Sentivist	NFR Security	http://www.nfr.com/solutions/support.php
Snort	Sourcefire	http://www.snort.org/dl/
Sourcefire	Sourcefire	http://www.sourcefire.com/services/support.html
StealthWatch	Lancope	http://www.lancope.com/customers/
StoneGate	StoneSoft Corporation	http://www.stonesoft.com/support/
Strata Guard	StillSecure	http://www.stillsecure.com/strataguard/support/updates.php
UnityOne	TippingPoint Technologies	http://www.tippingpoint.com/support.html
V-Secure	V-Secure Technologies, Inc.	http://www.v-secure.com/support/packages_bundles.asp

Common Enterprise Antivirus and Antispyware Software[41]

Web Site	URL
Central Command Vexira AntiVirus	
Downloads	http://www.centralcommand.com/downloads.html
Latest Version Numbers	http://www.centralcommand.com/versions.html
Support	http://www.centralcommand.com/support.html
Computer Associates eTrust Antivirus	
Computer Associates Security Advisory	http://www3.ca.com/securityadvisor/
Computer Associates Support	http://www3.ca.com/support/
Computer Associates Virus Information Center	http://www3.ca.com/securityadvisor/virusinfo/default.aspx
F-Secure Anti-Virus	
F-Secure Radar	http://www.f-secure.com/products/radar/
F-Secure Security Information Center	http://www.f-secure.com/virus-info/
F-Secure Support	http://support.f-secure.com/enu/home/
Lavasoft Ad-Aware	
Download, Support, Upgrade Center	http://www.lavasoftusa.com/
Microsoft Windows AntiSpyware (Beta)	
Using Microsoft Windows AntiSpyware (Beta)	http://www.microsoft.com/athome/security/spyware/software/howto/default.mspx
Network Associates McAfee VirusScan	
Downloads	http://www.mcafee.com/us/downloads/default.asp
McAfee AVERT Alerts	http://vil.nai.com/vil/content/alert.htm
McAfee AVERT Virus Information Library	http://vil.nai.com/vil/default.asp
Sophos Anti-Virus	
Download Latest Virus Identity Files	http://www.sophos.com/downloads/ide/
Sophos Email Notification	http://www.sophos.com/virusinfo/notifications/
Sophos Virus Analyses	http://www.sophos.com/virusinfo/analyses/
Spybot-Search & Destroy	

---

[41] This table lists some of the most popular antivirus and antispyware products. For information on other products, see the listing at the Virus Bulletin Web site located at http://www.virusbtn.com/resources/links/index.xml?ven.

Web Site	URL
Downloads	http://www.safer-networking.org/en/download/index.html
Support	http://www.safer-networking.org/en/support/index.html
Symantec AntiVirus	
Symantec Downloads	http://www.symantec.com/downloads/
Symantec Support	http://www.symantec.com/techsupp/
Symantec Security Response—Search and Latest Virus Threats Page	http://securityresponse.symantec.com/avcenter/vinfodb.html
Symantec Security Response—Alerting Offerings	http://securityresponse.symantec.com/avcenter/alerting_offerings.html
Trend Micro Anti-Spyware and VirusWall	
Support	http://kb.trendmicro.com/solutions/search/default.asp
Trend Micro Virus Encyclopedia Search	http://www.trendmicro.com/vinfo/virusencyclo/
Trend Micro Newsletters	http://www.trendmicro.com/subscriptions/default.asp

Other Common Security Applications

Product Line	Vendor	URL
Anti-Spam Servers		
Anti-Spam SMTP Proxy (ASSP) Server	ASSP Server Project	http://sourceforge.net/project/showfiles.php?group_id=69172
BitDefender AntiSpam for Mail Servers	Softwin	http://www.bitdefender.com/site/Main/view/Server-Products-Updates.html
GFiMailEssentials	GFI Software	http://support.gfi.com/
Kaspersky Anti-Spam	Kaspersky	http://www.kaspersky.com/productupdates/
MailShield Server	Lyris Technologies	http://www.lyris.com/store/mailshield/server/upgrade.html?s=sdbr
McAfee SPAMkiller	Network Associates	http://www.mcafee.com/us/downloads/default.asp
Merak Instant Anti Spam	Merak	http://www.merakmailserver.com/Download/
MIMEsweeper	Clearswift	http://www.clearswift.com/support/msw/patch.aspx
NetIQ MailMarshal	NetIQ	http://www.netiq.com/support/default.asp
SPAMfighter	SPAMfighter	http://www.spamfighter.com/Tutorial_Update.asp
Personal Firewalls and Suites		
BlackIce	Internet Security Systems	http://blackice.iss.net/update_center/
F-Secure Internet Security 2005	F-Secure	http://support.f-secure.com/enu/home/
Kaspersky Anti-Hacker	Kaspersky Labs	http://www.kaspersky.com/productupdates
Kerio Personal Firewall	Kerio Technologies	http://www.kerio.com/kpf_download.html
McAfee Personal Firewall Plus	Networks Associates Technology, Inc.	http://download.mcafee.com/us/upgradeCenter/?cid=11536

Product Line	Vendor	URL
Norton Personal Firewall	Symantec	http://www.symantec.com/downloads/
Panda Platinum Internet Security	Panda Software	http://www.pandasoftware.com/download/
PC-cillin Internet Security	Trend Micro	http://www.trendmicro.com/download/product.asp?productid=32
Sygate Personal Firewall	Sygate	http://smb.sygate.com/download_buy.htm
Tiny Firewall	Tiny Software	http://www.tinysoftware.com/home/tiny2?s=5375286922906826215A1&&pg=content05&an=tf6_download&cat=cat_tf6
ZoneAlarm	Zone Labs	http://download.zonelabs.com/bin/free/information/zap/releaseHistory.html
VPN Clients		
Cisco VPN Client	Cisco	http://www.cisco.com/public/sw-center/
NetScreen-Remote	Juniper	http://www.juniper.net/customers/support/
Nortel VPN Client	Nortel	http://www130.nortelnetworks.com/cgi-bin/eserv/cs/main.jsp?cscat=software&tranProduct=10621
ProSafe VPN Client	Netgear	http://kbserver.netgear.com/downloads_support.asp
SafeNet SoftRemote	CyberGuard	http://www.cyberguard.com/support/
VPN-1 SecuRemote, SecureClient	CheckPoint	http://www.checkpoint.com/downloads/index.html
Wireless IDS/IPS		
AirDefense	AirDefense	http://www.airdefense.net/support/
AirMagnet	AirMagnet	http://www.airmagnet.com/support/index.htm
AiroPeek	WildPackets	http://www.wildpackets.com/support/downloads
AirPatrol	Cirond	http://www.cirond.com/support.php
BlueSecure	BlueSocket	http://www.bluesocket.com/products/intrusionprotection.html
Highwall	Highwall Technologies	http://www.highwalltech.com/support.cfm
Red-Detect	Red-M	http://www.red-m.com/Support/
RFprotect	Network Chemistry	http://www.networkchemistry.com/support/
SpectraGuard	AirTight Networks	http://www.airtightnetworks.net/support/support_overview.html

General Vulnerability Management Resources

Resource Name	URL
US-CERT National Cyber Alert System	http://www.us-cert.gov/cas/
US-CERT National Vulnerability Database	http://nvd.nist.gov/
US-CERT Vulnerability Notes Database	http://www.kb.cert.org/vuls/
Open Source Vulnerability Database	http://www.osvdb.org/
SecurityFocus Vulnerability Database	http://www.securityfocus.com/vulnerabilities

Appendix E—Index

A

Accreditation, B-1
Administrative access, B-1
Application, B-1
Application configuration, 3-3
Authenticity, 2-10, 2-13, C-1
Automated inventory management tool, 2-5
Automated patch deployment, 2, 2-2, 2-16, 6-1
Automatic application update, 2, 2-3, 2-16, 6-1
Availability, B-1

B

Backdoor, 4-7
Backup, 2-11, 4-7, B-1

C

Certification, B-1
Common Vulnerabilities and Exposures, 5-1, 5-2
Compromise, 2-12, 4-7
Confidentiality, B-1
Configuration adjustment, 2-11, B-1
Cost, 3-4, 3-7
Cyber Security Alerts, 5-1
Cyber Security Bulletins, 5-1
Cyber Security Tips, 5-1

E

Enterprise patch and vulnerability management tool, 3-4, 3-5
Enterprise patch management tool, ES-2, ES-3, 2-1, 2-2, 2-8, 2-11, 3-8, 4-1, 4-7, C-4
    Agent-based, 4-1, C-5
    Non-agent-based, 4-1, C-5
Exploit code, ES-1, B-1, C-4

F

False negative, 3-8
False positive, 3-8
Federal Information Processing Standard 199, 2-5, 2-6
Firewall, B-1

H

Host, B-1
Hotfix, B-1

I

ICAT, 5-2
Incident response, 4-7
Information distribution, ES-2, 2-2, 2-13
Integrity, B-1
Inventory. *See* System inventory

L

Log, 2-13, 2-14
Log analysis tool, 3-5

M

Malicious code, 2-9, 2-10, 4-3
Manual patching, ES-3, 4-1, 4-5, 4-7
Metrics, ES-3, 3-1
    Development, 3-1
    Program implementation, 3-8
Misconfiguration, B-1
Mitigation
    Response time, 3-3

N

National Cyber Alert System. *See* United States Computer Emergency Readiness Team National Cyber Alert System
National Vulnerability Database, 3-2, 4-6, 5-1, 5-2
Network service, 3-2

O

Open Vulnerability Assessment Language, 5-2
Operating system, B-1

P

Patch, ES-1, 2-10, 2-11, 3-2, 4-7, 4-8, 6-1, B-1, C-1
    Deployment, 3-3, 6-1
Patch and vulnerability group, ES-2, 2-1, 2-15, 3-4, 6-1
Patch and vulnerability management, ES-1
    Process, 2-1
    Program, 2-15, 3-5, 6-1
        Maturity, 3-5
Patch log. *See* Log
Patch management tool. *See* Enterprise patch management tool
Performance, 3-7
Prioritization, ES-2, 2-2, 2-5, 2-8, 2-16, 6-1
Purchasing, 4-5, 4-8

R

Remediation, ES-1, ES-2, 2-2, 2-7, 2-9, 2-11, 6-1, B-1
    Database, ES-2, 2-2, 2-9, 2-16, 6-1
    Deployment, 2-2, 6-1
    Plan, 2-14, B-2
    Verification, 2-13, 2-16, 6-1
Risk, B-2

S

Security Configuration Checklists Program for IT Products, 4-5
Security plan, B-2
Security risks, 4-3, 4-7
Security source monitoring, ES-2, 2-2, 2-6, 2-7, 2-15, 3-3, 6-1, C-1
Software inventory, 4-4
Software removal, 2-11
Standardized configurations, ES-3, 2-1, 4-6, 4-8, 6-1
System, 2-3, 2-5, 3-1, B-2
System administrators, ES-1, 2-3, 3-4, B-2
System inventory, ES-2, 2-2, 2-3, 2-6, 2-15, 6-1
System owner, B-2

T

Testing, ES-2, 2-1, 2-2, 2-9, 2-16, 3-3, 6-1
Threat, 2-7, 2-8, 2-12, B-2
Training, ES-2, 2-3, 2-15, 2-16, 6-1

U

United States Computer Emergency Readiness Team, 5-1
    National Cyber Alert System, 5-1
    Vulnerability Notes Database, 5-2

V

Vendor security information, 2-8, C-1
Virtual local area network, 2-15
Virus, B-2
Vulnerability, ES-1, 1-1, 2-7, 2-8, 3-2, 4-5, 4-8, 5-1, B-2
    Database, 2-7, 2-8, 3-5, 5-2, C-4
    Mailing list, 2-8
    Scanning, ES-2, 2-3, 2-7, 2-13, 3-5, 3-8, 4-4, C-3
Vulnerability Notes Database. *See* United States Computer Emergency Readiness Team Vulnerability Notes Database

W

Workaround, B-2
Worm, B-2